Finding

Santiago

Finding Santiago

*Stories From and About
the Camino de Santiago*

Don Thomas

Table of Contents

Introduction

What I Intend This To Be About and Revised Edition Comments

"You know, you should really write a book, your stories are all so fascinating." Over the past several years, more and more people have said that to me after hearing me tell one or more of the stories in this book. After a few years, I started telling people they would have to wait for the book so they could read all my stories.

When I first discovered the Camino de Santiago in 2012, I never intended to take it this far. Writing a book was the furthest thing from my mind. When I was asked why I was doing the Camino de Santiago, I would always reply, "For various reasons." I did not have only one driving reason.

Although I am a "Cradle Catholic" born into that faith tradition, it was not my faith alone that induced me to do a Camino. I suppose it was a combination of wanderlust combined with a small sense of adventure and an element of religion that caused me to make my decision to do my first Camino in 2013.

Since 2013, I have had the privilege and honor to meet many wonderful people from all over the world either while on my personal pilgrimages on the Camino de Santiago or working as a volunteer at the Pilgrim Office in Santiago de Compostela. Through these interactions, things happened. Sometimes these things were very poignant and sad. Other times they were extremely funny. But all of them were very meaningful to me. The stories in this book are all true.

My association with the Camino de Santiago literally changed the trajectory of my life. I went from being a retired "couch potato" to being actively involved in planning and walking my Caminos, helping others to benefit from my experiences, and ultimately, to actually volunteering to work face-to-face with pilgrims from all over the world arriving at Santiago de Compostela.

Along the way, a thought began to take root in my mind. The thought was that there must be some hidden, existential meaning or purpose to be learned by making this pilgrimage. Each day, I wondered, I thought, I mediated, then I thought some more. Frankly, I am still pondering.

It took many attempts and several years of trying to answer the simple question – WHY? Finally, I gave up trying. Then, in 2019, the answer finally dawned on me. It was one of those lightbulb moments that everyone has. The clouds part, the light in our brain switches on, and we have an "Ah HA moment."

The revelation to me, after all my experiences, pains, suffering and exhilarations along the way, was that the purpose of the Camino de Santiago was to make me a better person. This realization cut across all aspects of thought and behavior. It touched my inner sense of self, my acceptance of differences with others, my personal obsessions, idiosyncrasies and quirks, as well as how I interacted with others.

Then, I got metaphysical and wondered if this did not have something to do with the "cult of Santiago." This is the entire paradigm and environment that surrounds the life of the Apostle Saint James the Greater, his death, transition / transfer to burial under the Cathedral, and the eventual focal point of pilgrimage for millions of people from every corner of the globe. I wondered if this might not indirectly be the aura or spirit of the Saint working through each of us who make the journey.

That is when I decided that, if and when I wrote the book – this book – my purpose would be to explore the effects on what

I might have experienced or achieved through my Camino-related activities. This would literally be my search for Santiago. After rolling this around for some months, I decided to name the book *"Finding Santiago."* I did this because my goal was to explore all of my experiences to see whether or not I could come to any worthwhile conclusions at the end of the storytelling.

What this book is not, is a "How to Do the Camino" book. There are many other fine books like this. I need not go there. It is a not a guidebook to the Camino de Santiago. That category has been thoroughly done as well. It does not need one more person's opinions.

Neither is this a book about MY Caminos. One of the first things I learned from my pilgrimages was that each pilgrim does his or her own Camino. There have been dozens or more books, where a pilgrim recounts their experience on THEIR Camino. Finally, this is not a motivational book that tries to speak to your inner, spiritual being. There are many such books relating to the Camino de Santiago.

And here it is. This is a compendium of my stories, that I witnessed or participated in on my efforts at *Finding Santiago*. To better clarify the context of each story, I am including in the title of each chapter or story either (P) or (V) to tell the reader if this story occurred while I was a pilgrim (P) and walking, or at Santiago, and working as a volunteer (V). I hope this helps you understand the context for the story better.

Lastly, I sincerely hope you find my stories interesting and perhaps even amusing. My purpose is to entertain, amuse, inform and, in a small way, perhaps motivate you to consider doing the Camino de Santiago and *Finding Santiago…*

Comment on this revised edition:

Finding Santiago was first published in July 2020. Full editing was not done – in a rush to get the book published before the author was supposed to go to Spain to work as a volunteer. The global COVID pandemic stopped that. While nearly all reviews of this book have been positive, some have pointed out that there were numerous editorial mistakes. Friends of the author have explained that missing accents are viewed as spelling errors in the Spanish language. The author simply wants to ensure that this book represents his full and best efforts. No new material is added. No existing material was removed. The original manuscript has been revised to remove errors.

1

Finding Santiago
Northern Virginia, USA

October 2012 (P)

By October 2012, I had been officially retired for over five years. My wife and I returned from living in Belgium for two years in 2008. Since returning home to our very nice condominium in Northern Virginia, I had not been doing much of anything. My days were consumed with spending a lot of time on the internet, corresponding with friends, and fairly regular walks. Nothing long or strenuous mind you.

I knew that I needed physical exercise. I undertook to do errands by foot whenever possible. Fortunately, most of the shops I needed on a daily basis were within a 20-minute walk, slightly more than one mile. The terrain is fairly flat with low rolling hills. It is often called "horse country." Although we were living in a planned community, where most all the greenery was installed during construction.

By contrast, my wife took up the study and practice of yoga with a vengeance. She became very good at it, and even competitive with her fellow practitioners. Her practice had her taking several classes each week at a studio down the road from our home.

One such occasion was on a Saturday afternoon in October 2012. While my wife was out doing her yoga thing, I was 'couch surfing' in my living room in front of my television. Basically, this means I was comfortably reclining on the sofa using the remote control to 'surf' though the hundreds of channels casting about for something to occupy my brain.

As I was doing this, I hit on one of the several Public Broadcasting System (PBS) channels we had available to us. In the metropolitan Washington D.C. area, I recall that we had at least three such channels.

As I hit on this one channel there was a title page for a Rick Steves' "Europe through the Back Door" travel program. This one was entitled *Galicia and the Camino de Santiago*. Hmm, I thought. I have been watching and collecting DVDs on this series for most every show Rick has produced, but I do not recall seeing this one. I got comfortable and watched it.

Basically, the program was a once over lightly description of the Camino Francés, from Saint Jean Pied de Port in the foothills of the Pyrenees in southern France, to the Cathedral in Santiago de Compostela in Galicia, Spain. From the opening scenes in Saint Jean Pied de Port, I was riveted to the program.

As an introduction to Rick Steves for those of you not living in the United States, this fellow has made a wonderful career of traveling through and across all of Europe, making 30-minute travel programs. His purpose is to cause others to become interested in his passion, traveling throughout Europe, meeting new people, eating new and different food, experiencing different cultures and languages. He has been doing this for over 40 years. When my wife and I traveled to Europe several times annually, we would usually base our activities on his very good series of guide books.

Residing near Seattle, Washington, Rick has built a small but successful travel-based empire. He sells DVRs of his programs, produces a wide variety of tour guides and maps, sells a wide variety of travel accessories, and has even developed his own travel agency for planning trips.

Sometimes, I think he has the best job in the world. He spends some four months each year on the road, mostly in Europe, with a cameraperson and a producer gathering video footage and information to produce more and new programs. He lives out of his own-design travel backpack suitcase.

Anyway, back to *Finding Santiago*. As I was watching this program, I developed the sense that this was something very interesting that I might aspire to. I mentioned earlier that in retirement I was not doing anything much in particular with my life. As there were no pauses for commercial adverts and as I did not have paper nearby, I wrote "Camino de Santiago" on my forearm.

Thirty minutes later the program was over. I immediately went to my computer and fired up the Google browser. Searching for "Camino de Santiago" brought back over 300,000 results. Yikes! This suggested there might be something to this entire notion.

One of the top-ranked results was a Wikipedia article titled "The Way of St. James." Okay, I knew Santiago meant Saint James in Spanish, so I clicked on it. Well, that was the Rosetta Stone for me. After reading the article several times, I proceeded to devour the references and "for further information" links at the bottom of the article. There were quite a few onward references.

I spent the next two days obsessively drilling down and following every reference and link to this Wikipedia article. Among the most important findings for me were:

- American Pilgrims on the Camino (APOC) – <u>www.americanpilgrims.org</u>

- The Camino de Santiago internet forum – <u>www.caminodesantiago.me</u>

- Cathedral of Santiago de Compostela – <u>http://</u> <u>catedraldesantiago.es/</u>

There were many, many other links to other organizations and resources. Among the more significant were links to the 2010 film *The Way*. At that time, we were members of the Netflix DVR by mail service. Being curious, I immediately added *The Way* to my Netflix wish list moving it to a top priority.

The DVR arrived about a week later. I watched it twice, totally engrossed, before asking my wife to watch it with me once. After that, I told her that I was TOTALLY going to do this. She thought I was crazy. Never, at 59 years of age, mostly sedentary, and in over 30 years of marriage have I ever been that determined about anything. I think she humored me. I watched it two more times.

Then things started getting serious. I joined the American Pilgrims on the Camino and started mining their website for information. I also joined the Camino de Santiago online forum and started asking questions, doing searches and getting answers to the classic: "who, what, when, where, why and how" questions. Now I knew the scope, beginning and end of my planned journey.

I also learned through seeking and searching that the seminal guidebook seemed to be John Brierley's "*A Pilgrims Guide to the Camino de Santiago*." I ordered one right away. It arrived some days later and provided a very valuable foundation and framework for future planning.

Now, I knew where I was going to start, end, and generally stay each day. The Brierley book provided that framework. Between the APOC and Camino Forum websites, I began to develop a list of the equipment or gear I would need. I owned nothing suitable to purpose, except for my Ex Officio boxer shorts that I had been wearing while I traveled globally for decades.

I made a list, checked it twice, and with much learned from the online forums, made the first of many trips to my local REI store. This is Recreational Equipment Inc. and is a cooperative, based near Seattle, Washington, that has been providing outdoor gear for decades. They have branches all over the United States. In Canada, there is a similar outfitter called MEC (Mountain Equipment Cooperative) www.mec.ca.

Having learned that properly fitted footwear and a rucksack were the most important bits of gear I would need, I started with the footwear. I was fortunate to find an REI salesperson who was an experienced thru-hiker (long distance wilderness hiking). He had heard about the Camino de Santiago, but did not know anyone who had actually done it. I shared with him what I had learned from the forums about wearing two pair of non-cotton socks, and how to allow enough space in the correct dimensions to avoid foot problems on the trail.

His practical experience and my input from the forums led me to buy my first pair of hiking boots. I chose the Keen Targhee II mid-high, Gore Tex-lined boots. Both the salesperson and I agreed that this would offer the comfort needed as well as the support I would need when carrying 25 – 30 pounds on my back for a month or more. I am NOT a petite person and have always had weak ankles. The salesperson even knew to go online to the Keen website (http://www.keenfootware.com/) to determine if this particular boot ran small or large. According to Keen, this model ran one-half size small at the time.

Working from my street shoe size, at the time a US size 11 medium width, we pulled two pair of socks off the shelves (I was going to buy them anyway) and put them on. The first pair were microfiber liner socks, very thin and intended to wick moisture from my feet and reduce friction. The second pair of socks were a Smartwool merino nylon blend to provide cushioning and insulation. When on, my feet then measured sized US 11.5, up half a size.

The salesperson then asked me if my feet generally swelled at the end of the day. I said yes, so he added one more half-size to his 11.5 calculation. Now we were up to a US sized 12 foot.

Finally, he told me that, from his years of experience distance thru-hiking the Appalachian Trail and Pacific Crest Trail, his feet tended to splay or grow up to half a size after walking a month or more with a loaded pack and in hiking boots all day. This idea has been mentioned on at least one of the forums, and we agreed to add a final one-half size to my original US sized 11 foot.

We finally arrived at a technical calculation that I needed a US sized 12.5 boot. This was 1.5 sizes larger than my street shoe size. As he had already found out that this model boot ran one half size smaller than indicated (12.5), he settled on a US size 13 Keen boot – YIKES! Any larger and I would be into clown shoe territory!

They fit like a glove. I have worn this model boot ever since, and have them resoled when the outsole wears down, at least until the upper boot or inner liner starts to shred. You can easily find a vendor that does hiking boot resoling by doing an online search for this service. I found that the outsoles last about 1,000 km before they need resoling. Your experience may vary. My first pair of Keen boots went through two resoling operations and nearly 3,000 km, over four Caminos, before the uppers said, "Enough already." I am now on my second pair of the exact boots.

The takeaway on footwear is that everyone has different feet. I even have two feet that are not symmetrical. I was born that way. What works for me or for any other person may not work for you. The key is to take the time to get the proper fit with the exact socks you plan to wear, and allowing for the other factors discussed above, if they pertain to you.

Now I had my properly fitted footwear, I started to wear them on my local errand walks to get them broken in. I then started training by walking to some destination. These walks were most always on paved surfaces, generally blacktop / macadam. As mentioned in my introduction, exercise for the sake of exercise, or because it is a good thing, or walking for exercise never appealed to me, ever. Knowing I had to practice to improve my ability to walk in heavy hiking boots and with a backpack, I had to have a destination. I needed a reason to walk from point A to B and back again.

I used my car to chart out several routes that always either ended at a coffee shop or supermarket. This would allow me to combine a daily errand as a reason for walking. One route was a total of 3 miles (5 km) round trip. The other was 5 miles one way (8 km). By walking these routes, I could walk up to a 5 or 16 km round trip. I did this first with only boots and a water bottle, then eventually with a rucksack. This eventually became a daily routine. Treating myself to a latte and cookie as a reward.

The second major investment that I, and any intending pilgrim will make, is a good quality, properly fitted rucksack. I returned to the same REI shop and salesperson for help. He had another salesperson assist with using a plastic fitting frame to determine how long my torso was and to recommend various makes, models, and volumes of rucksacks available in my torso size. After discussion of my planned journey, we settled on an Osprey Kestrel 48-liter rucksack in a Medium / Long Torso size.

They loaded the rucksack with 25 pounds of sandbags and had me walk around the store for 30 minutes wearing the boots I had purchased some weeks earlier. They wanted to determine the comfort, adjusting the various straps and showing me how to do it properly to spread the load correctly, use the hip-band system as it was designed, and to further test the fit of my boots.

They even had a fiberglass modeled "mountain" that allowed you to simulate walking up and downhill to determine how the weight of the rucksack affected your feet, especially when coming downhill. One of the most seriously wrong things that too many people do is to buy their footwear too small, or not adjust the laces properly so that on a downhill, the toes strike the inside of the toe box. This is the most common cause of toe blisters, loss of toenails and "black toe."

By the end of this two-stage process, we jointly determined that I had the properly fitted footwear and rucksack for undertaking the Camino de Santiago.

This was the easy bit.

Once I got the properly fitted rucksack home, I filled it with plastic bags of new kitty litter. It is good that we owned two cats at the time, so it would not be wasted. I put a total of 24 pounds in the rucksack for weight and then added a bed pillow to 'fill' the remaining volume to give the rucksack shape. I proceeded to wear this rucksack on several weekly walks. I wanted to be sure it was adjusted properly and carried a simulated load as intended. Walking with a loaded rucksack is more difficult than walking without any rucksack. But, over some weeks I got used to it. It is a good thing that Northern Virginia has four seasons and we were going into winter…

After reading the Brierley guide and going back and forth on the forums, I determined that I should schedule my Camino to start at Saint Jean Pried de Port at the end of April 2013. I wanted to avoid the Easter rush I had read about, most of the snow in the Pyrenees Mountains, and wanted more sunny days. As it was already December, 2012, this gave me about four months to get ready.

I started buying gear I thought I would use based on advice in the forums. There was a LOT that I did not know, and would learn only after trial and error.

In early January 2013, I kicked things up a notch by buying my air tickets to lock down my plans. Living near Washington – Dulles International Airport made this easy. I booked an "open jaw" flight from Washington to Paris, with a return from Madrid. I then used Rail Europe (https://www.raileurope-world.com/) to buy a TGV ticket to travel from Gare Montparnasse in Paris to Saint Jean Pied de Port. I used the ALSA bus website https://www.alsa.es/ to buy a return bus ticket from Santiago de Compostela to Madrid.

Using the Brierley guidebook and www.booking.com, I proceeded to make a hotel reservation at Saint Jean Pied de Port for the first two nights before starting out. I also made a hotel reservation in Madrid for the night before my planned flight home. I would take the ALSA bus, stay near the airport, and be able to check-in easily for my return flight. My thought at the time was to stay in albergues while on Camino, like all the others, or so I thought.

By the end of January 2013, I was committed. I had my footwear, rucksack, and was obtaining the suggested gear indicated. Moreover, I had locked down my travel to and from the Camino's starting and ending points. I continued to take my local walks, and read as much as I could find about the adventure I was about to undertake.

My final advance efforts to plan, were to schedule visits with all my regular doctors to make sure I was healthy. I had an annual physical, dental checkup, vision exam and new eyeglasses, and consulted a podiatrist about custom insoles for my boots. In the end, he recommended sturdy Superfeet insoles. I bought the stiff, heavy-duty green type.

By the end of February 2013, I was certifiably healthy, geared-up and focusing on researching everything about Saint James the Greater – Santiago. In the process of getting this far, I had answered these important considerations:

- What I was going to do – walk the traditional Camino Francés

- When was I going to do it – from the last week in April 2013

- Where I was doing it – St. Jean Pied de Port to Santiago de Compostela

- How I was going to accomplish it – one step at a time… all the way

I still needed to suitably answer the "who" was Santiago really, and "why" am I doing this? The first question, or who Santiago was is something I started reading about and, seven years later am still learning more. The "why" did not come to me until much later, but I now understand it very well.

2

First Steps, Oh My!
Saint Jean Pied de Port, France

April 2013 (P)

Here I am, staying in a nice small hotel in the center of Saint Jean Pied de Port, the traditional starting point for the Camino Francés route. I arrived by local train from Bayonne, where the TGV from Paris – Gare Montparnasse left me. I transferred at Bayonne to the TER #62 route, a local train, to get to Saint Jean Pied de Port.

The ride up to the foothills of the Pyrenees Mountains is absolutely beautiful. It took about 90 minutes in a light-rail vehicle. Virtually all of the other people on this single car articulated train were pilgrims. The car had rucksacks and bicycles all over the place. The train was full, but it appeared everyone was headed to the same place.

Although there were several intermediate stops along the way up into the hills, few people got off, and no one got on. It turns out that Saint Jean Pied de Port is the actual end of the rail line. It was impossible to get lost.

On arrival at Saint Jean, everyone got off the train and wandered into town. I knew where I had reservations and I headed there to check-in. My hotel was in the center of the main street in the old section, Rue de la Citadelle. The castle or Citadelle is at the top of the street, and the old gate leading out from the town through the ancient stone walls surrounding this town to the Camino is at the opposite lower end.

From my research, I knew I had to check in at the local Pilgrim Office, as well as to arrange for a suitcase to be transported to Santiago to await my arrival. I knew that I had two nights and the day in between to relax, experience Saint Jean, complete my provisioning and buy souvenirs. That first evening, I had a wonderful locally caught trout dinner in a local restaurant. The wine was not at all bad either.

The next day, I wandered all over the town taking photos and playing tourist. Along the way, I stopped into the Pilgrim Office at #39 Rue de la Citadelle to get my APOC-provided pilgrim passport or credencial stamped – my first stamp (sello) on the Camino… yippee!

At the Pilgrim Office, they were very helpful and provided a current briefing on conditions over the Napoleón Pass to Roncesvalles. Also, they gave me printed copies of the complete elevation profile for the Camino Francés, as well as lists of albergues along the way, and answered any question I asked.

I did ask them to call the Refuge Orisson to confirm my reservation for the following night's stay. They were VERY accommodating. Finally, and not insignificantly, I obtained my first ever concha – a large scallop shell with a string. This is the symbol of a pilgrim on the Camino de Santiago. This shell was attached to the outside of my rucksack, where it rode for the next five weeks. Later, I learned these shells were the leftovers from Coquilles St. Jacques at local restaurants.

I asked the hotel proprietor to call Express Bourricot (http:// www.expressbourricot.com/) to confirm they would pick up my small suitcase the next morning after my departure take it to Santiago, store it securely at the Albergue Hostal Lasalle where it would await my arrival. Payment was left in an envelope with logistical details and contact information.

Chapter 2

After buying espadrille shoes for all the women in my family, obtaining some last-minute snacks, bottled water, and even buying a new Ferrino hiking raincoat - poncho in the local outdoors store, I was almost ready to go.

As a side note, espadrille shoes are a local Basque handicraft. They have been making these shoes by hand and selling them for centuries. There are several shops, all selling locally made canvas, rope and rubber espadrilles. Do not miss them.

At my hotel, I packed the bag I was to send ahead to Santiago, including all the espadrilles I bought, and proceeded to have another great local meal. This was followed at 8:00 pm by the pilgrim Mass at the local church at the bottom of Rue de la Citadelle, on the left, shortly before the bridge over the river.

The Mass was wonderful. Apparently, there were several priests from around the world, including one from South Korea, who concelebrated the Mass. The Mass was in French. I retain enough of my basic French to get the idea. After the Mass, there was a special Pilgrim Blessing for all those pilgrims who would be starting out the next morning.

Back to the hotel for the last night before starting out. I unpacked and repacked my rucksack and double-checked the send-ahead suitcase. Considering the adventure I was about to undertake I slept remarkably well.

The takeaway from this experience is that it is worthwhile to stay two nights in a hotel before you start out. Saint Jean Pied de Port is a beautiful little French town with friendly and helpful people. As the main celebrant at the Pilgrim Mass stated the night before, this town has been preparing and sending pilgrims off to Santiago de Compostela for more than 1,100 years.

Tweedle Dee and Tweedle Dum

Saint Jean Pied de Port, France

April 2013 (P)

The next morning brought bright blue skies with only a few clouds. It was chilly, but I had planned for that with a proper fleece zip-up jacket. I finished breakfast at the hotel, settled my bill, deposited the suitcase for onward shipping, and bid farewell to Saint Jean Pied de Port.

I walked down the Rue de la Citadelle past the church over the bridge, then up the hill to the exit gate through the old stone walls. Just across the street opposite the gate there was a sign, the left pointing to the Napoleón Pass, and the right towards the alternative route via Valcarlos. To the left I proceeded.

As soon as I started, or after the bridge downtown, there started a continual up-slope. After exiting the town and taking the left at the fork in the road, the slope increased slightly.

HAH! Although I had read quite a lot about this first segment from Saint Jean, I was not prepared for the reality. The route continues on mostly paved town streets, through residential areas for a while before becoming rural and agricultural. However, the up-slope continues... and continues... and continues. It did not look this difficult in the movie *The Way*.

This slope does not necessarily become steeper. It just continues. Once the paved roads end and the farm tracks appear, the slope continues. At times, it seems to level off only to resume 50 meters later. After 30 minutes of this, I am starting to question my wisdom.

After one hour, my breathing becomes more labored. Each breath is harder and harder to take. THEN it dawns on me. I am walking UP into the Pyrenees Mountains! I started at some elevation in the foothills, but then continued to walk up, and up. It then dawned on me that I was climbing the mountains, while making nice with the horses, sheep and goats I came across. That is when I started enforcing a mandatory stop to catch my breath and water break every 30 minutes whether I was thirsty or not.

I knew that I had a bed reserved and confirmed at the private albergue Refuge Orisson. I knew that this was about 8 kilometers from Saint Jean Pied de Port. I just had to get there – alive!

The reason for staying only 8 kilometers from my starting point is that the entire first stage according to Brierley was about 27 km. It occurred to me early on that I ought not take too big a bite my first day out as I had never done anything like this before. It turned out to be a VERY wise decision.

This being my first Camino, I had no concept of what my normal walking pace might be. I would come to learn that it was 3 / 4 / 5. This is 3 kilometers per hour uphill, 4 kilometers per hour on level or rolling terrain, and 5 kilometers per hour on a sustained downhill segment. I have since come to learn to look at a map or guide, look at the distance to be covered and divide by 4 for a rough estimate of the time it is going to take me to cover the distance the next day.

I just knew it was taking me forever to get up this hill. After about 90 minutes, other pilgrims who had started after me were overtaking me. Some of them stopped to ask me if I were okay. You see, by this time, my normal progression was to walk for 30 seconds or a minute, then stop, bend over and hack my lungs up. The coughing was monumental. Some of the well-meaning passers-by went away satisfied with a wave, and the now learned 'Buen Camino' or 'Bon Chemin' in French.

I started telling folks, between hacking coughs, that I was fine, just waiting for Tweedle Dee and Tweedle Dum to catch up to me. Everyone got quizzical at that statement, and some must have thought me delirious.

I would take as best a breath I could, and in between heaving breaths explain that these were my two lungs, Tweedle Dee and Tweedle Dum. They were each a squishy red muscular bag with short legs and tiny feet, and were finding getting up this hill very difficult. I must stop and wait for them to catch up. I would follow with the comment that they were being bores and slowing me down. We would have a laugh, then the clearly, better-breathing, other pilgrims would press on.

Then, about two hours after leaving Saint Jean, during one such doubled over hacking attack a couple of younger fellows stop. One placed a hand on my shoulder and asked: "How are you doing old man? Can you make it okay?"

Well, as I am hacking and coughing, I told this fellow in between hacking coughs that I was fine, thank you very much for asking, that I was merely waiting for my two lungs Tweedle Dee and Tweedle Dum to catch me up, and as soon as I can stand up, I am going to thrash you with these walking sticks…I AM NOT OLD! They were taken aback, wished me well and continued on.

Not 30 minutes later, I rounded a bend and there, a wonder to behold, was an oasis in the veritable desert, the Refuge Orisson. I had made it. I would live to suffer another day. I prayed for cold beer. I was rewarded.

4

My Kids are Gonna KILL Me!

Orisson, France

April 2013 (P)

I arrived at the Refuge Orisson, checked in, and was assigned a lower bunk bed in a space located under the deck across from the albergue building. This space had two showers, separate from the two sinks and two toilets. It was, as I would come to appreciate, very well organized. There were four double bunk beds in the sleeping room. Just outside, there was a clothes line for air drying clothing. I laid out my sleeping bag, did some hand washing, hung it on the line outside using clothespins (pegs) I had brought, and then walked up to the deck to start collecting on my hard-earned reward for almost crawling up that hill.

As I was settling in at a table in the sun, with million-dollar, jaw-droppingly beautiful views of the snowcapped Pyrenees Mountains in the distance to the north and east, I hear a woman speaking loudly to her friends in English going on about how her kids are going to kill her when they find out. As I am listening it becomes apparent that she has somehow lost her new iPhone in the eight kilometers from Saint Jean Pied de Port and here.

Me being me, I politely inquire if I can be of any help. Now I am getting the full excited story. It seems Vera (we shall call her Vera) is from Country Cork in Ireland. Only yesterday, before she departed Dublin, her adult children presented her with a new Apple iPhone.

They wanted to be certain they could both speak to and see, using Face Time, their mother, grandmother and great-grandmother as she went on her grand Camino adventure. As regards age, let's just say that Vera was on the far side of 70, but very youthful and spry.

The children even provided her with a pink and white Hello Kitty phone cover to protect the phone and so she would not lose it. Ha! They underestimated Vera. She had previously been using a flip-phone with almost none of the features of a smartphone. Vera was still very much in learning mode. Everything was new to her. She quickly got lost in all the available functions of the phone. Evidently, she became distracted.

Vera is convinced she had the phone when she left Saint Jean. She claimed to have taken many photos. In fact, she said she stopped for a break at a round concrete "thingie" a short distance before Refuge Orisson. From there, she said, you could see all the way to heaven. These were her words. But it was a very clear day, and I could share her enthusiasm for the views.

Now, this gets interesting. In my huffing and puffing my way up that eight-kilometer slope from Saint Jean, I too, passed the round concrete structure on the right. To me it appeared to be a cistern of some sort. It was perhaps three meters in diameter and at least two meters were projecting from the earth.

Except, when I passed it, I saw at the right-most edge, a piece of something that was definitely pink. I did not stop to investigate because: (1) pink is not a color I prefer, (2) I determined NOT to add effort by climbing up this cistern thing; and, (3) I was being very lazy at the time.

With the lightbulb flashing in my brain I say to Vera, "You know, in all my research about the historical Camino and reading many, many stories about pilgrimages, I have often read that miracles occur all along the Camino every day. In fact, I say, it is often said that Saint James – Santiago - works in strange ways. Another thing I learned is that if you need something, it mysteriously appears…"

By now, I am into my second pint of draft beer. I am comfortable, enjoying the views and chatting with the arriving pilgrims. Vera asks, "Do ya think it's possible?" My reply is, "Why don't you hop on back to that concrete thingie and just check? Nothing ventured nothing gained… I will watch your stuff and entertain your friends."

Vera heads BACK towards Saint Jean. The distance to the concrete cistern is only a few hundred meters but is around a bend in the road. As a result, we cannot see her after five minutes.

Twenty minutes later Vera comes trotting back to the table area waiving her pink and white Hello Kitty-clad iPhone in one hand. She gives me a big hug and states that I am her lucky leprechaun. Everyone assembled had a good chuckle as I am bigger than any two or three such mythical creatures. But I did tell her that if she finds the pot of gold next time, she has to split it with me.

I concluded by spotting a round for Vera and her two friends, and me of course. After that trial by elevation coming up to Orisson, I had earned it.

This was my first incarnation of two truisms I was to have reinforced again and again:

- Santiago does work in mysterious ways and sometimes his methods are just weird; and,

- On Camino, if you need something just say it to anyone nearby. Serendipity runs amuck on the Camino. Your needs will be met.

Trust me on this, it just works this way. I long ago stopped questioning how it works. Now I just marvel when it happens.

5

Can You Fix It?

Orisson, France

April 2013 (P)

I am still on my initial arrival at Refuge Orisson, having just walked eight kilometers up from Saint Jean Pied de Port. After a couple of hours, I am settled in, working on being very well hydrated. I am on my third pint of beer and am continuing to admire the views while chatting with the other pilgrims. We all agree that the first segment up from Saint Jean is a doozie.

Vera had found her phone and is thrilled. As I was passing time and doing some serious relaxing in the warm, late April sun, I saw a woman playing with a hiking pole. She is trying to adjust it, but it will not stay tightened. Other pilgrims have tried, without success, to tighten the two segments to maintain the length.

I noticed that the hiking pole is a Leki model. I happened to be using Leki hiking poles. Again, me being me, I ask if I might have a look at it. I introduce myself.

My new acquaintance is a woman named Michelle (that's what I will call her). She is from northern Florida near Orlando in the US. We exchange pleasantries and I offer her a glass of whatever while I am playing with her pole. She opts for red wine and we are getting comfortable.

Michelle explains she is very upset because these hiking poles belonged to her late husband, who passed 18 months earlier. They were both avid hikers and he used these poles to hike both classic long-distance US through hiking routes.

These routes included the Appalachian Trail (AT) and the Pacific Crest Trail (PCT). The former starts at Springer Mountain in Georgia, and runs 2,200 miles along the heavily forested Appalachian Mountain chain all the way up to Mount Kathadin in Maine. The latter is 2,650 miles long and starts at the border between the US and Mexico. It runs through mountains, deserts, hills, snow and blazing sun up to the border with Canada.

Michelle explains, with tears, that she and her late husband planned to do the Camino de Santiago together, but he passed suddenly before they could make the trip together. She was doing this Camino for him as much as for herself. Using his poles, wearing his ballcap and his scarf, it was like he was still with her. I understood exactly what she was saying.

As I am fiddling with her poles, I determine that two adjacent segments of one pole will not tighten to fix the desired pole length. Then I get a brilliant idea. I scurried downstairs to the bunk room to fetch one of my poles.

One of my earliest findings about hiking poles is that all of the twist-to-tighten or loosen segmented poles use a variation of a nylon expander collar. As you twist the two segments, the collar moves up or down a reverse-threaded bolt to expand outward to grip the inside surface of the pole or loosen to allow adjustment of the pole length.

As I am doing this, I am getting more background on my new Camino friend. She said that growing up, she always wanted to be a seamstress. But her parents would not hear of it. They forbade her to follow her dream, and insisted she find a professional job. As a result, Michelle spent her working years as a nurse.

However, after marrying, her husband liked to sail and

they bought a boat. To turn her dream avocation in to a reality, she installed a sewing machine on their apparently not small sailing boat. She went on to tell me how popular they were in any marina they moored in, once word got out that there was someone with a sewing machine who could make sail and other gear repairs. They made lots of sailing friends that way. To me, this was interesting but I filed it away in my messy brain.

Anyway, back to the drama of the hiking pole. I disassembled my Leki hiking pole and then did the same to hers, removing the same two adjacent segments. I immediately learned two things. The diameter size of the particular nylon adjuster collar is color-coded. All Leki 12 mm diameter collars are one color; all 14 mm diameter collars are another standard color, etc.

Being clever, I swapped our respective adjusting collars of the same color. That solved Michelle's problem immediately, making her pole fully adjustable. Putting her nylon adjuster collar on my pole made it not work, in the same manner that her pole was failing to adjust.

Now I knew exactly what the problem was. Over years of use, the nylon adjuster collar on Michelle's pole had been worn down. No matter how you turned it, either way, it would not expand enough to press against the inside of the pole tube to regulate the length. It would turn properly on the reverse threaded screw, but the nylon collar would no longer spread enough.

Once I returned my adjusting collar back to my pole and adjusted the length correctly for tomorrow, I turned my attention to Michelle's predicament. I explained what I learned to her, and told her that the correct fix was to go to an outdoor shop that sold hiking poles and which might have replacement parts.

By now, I had used the free Wi-Fi to check online determining that, yes, replacement parts were available. But, being in the middle of the Pyrenees Mountains, there were no outdoor shops in the offing. I needed a Plan B.

Enter duck tape (also called duct tape). Pilgrims ALWAYS carry duck tape. Over the decades, I have learned that the uses to which duck tape can be put are limited only by one's imagination and the available supply of tape. My plan was to try to thicken the worn adjuster collar with a few turns of tape to see if it would work.

Voila! I applied two turns of duck tape, torn lengthwise to make it thinner, reassembled the segments and adjusted it to Michelle's length, tightening it so it would not come loose.

I explained to her that this was a temporary fix, until she could replace the somewhat generic part that was worn. Until she could arrange for a replacement, she ought not loosen the segments for any reason, as they might not cooperate and tighten again.

Success! Michelle is thrilled! The assorted nearby pilgrims are impressed, and I am now being called Tom the Tinkerer. I am finding that I am deriving a huge degree of satisfaction whenever I can help another person. Plus, I have reconnected an absentminded pilgrim with her smartphone, and repaired a worn hiking pole.

Darn, that fourth beer went down easy! I let Michelle buy me one to say thank you.

6

My First Camino Family
Orisson, France

April 2013 (P)

One of the many unique things about the Camino de Santiago is the fact that many pilgrims associate with other pilgrims all heading in the same direction early on in their travel. This creates a shared bond. These folks tend to walk with each other most days, catching up with one another after breaks of several days, if individual plans changed, or someone wants or needs to stay an extra day someplace along the way. This is called your "Camino Family."

Most pilgrims tend to start their Camino from standard transportation nodes along the Camino Francés and other routes. These can be loosely defined as places where there are good rail and bus connections to other major cities. For example, along the Camino Francés, you can get to and from viable starting or ending places at Saint Jean Pied de Port, Pamplona, Logroño, Burgos, Sahagún, León, Astorga, Ponferrada, and Sarria. There may, and likely are, other viable starting or stopping nodes. But these are the major ones that I know of.

When several pilgrims all start at the same place on the same day, they just seem to form a group. The members of this group support and look after one another. If someone needs something, the others help to provide it. If one person has a problem, the others will typically pitch in to help sort it out.

At the Refuge Orisson, they have a long-practiced ritual for creating a pilgrim family. For most all pilgrims staying overnight, this is their first night out of Saint Jean Pied de Port. And for most of these pilgrims, this is their first ever foray on any Camino.

Each evening there is a group dinner served family style. The food is usually a simple one-pot stew or very thick soup. This filling main course is supplemented by fabulous French bread and bottomless red wine. Bottled water and soft drinks are also available.

This dinner is served family-style on very long rectangular tables where you sit next to and across from complete strangers. I had the advantage of speaking with some of these folks and helping at least two such pilgrims earlier in the day.

The ritual includes each of the several dozen pilgrims present standing up, giving their first name, where they are from, and briefly explaining why they are doing the Camino. I recall on my first time that there were more than 30 pilgrims present from all over the world. In fact, five of the six continents were represented: Europe, Asia, Africa, North and South America. Only Antarctica was not represented.

We each, in turn, gave our names, origin and purpose. This was fascinating as it also served as an icebreaker that induced complete strangers to speak with one another. Almost everyone had English as a second, or third language. Those that did not speak any English had new friends translate for them.

That is how I met Phil. I am using his true name for a reason that will become apparent later. Phil is a retired Methodist minister from near Liverpool, England. While only in his mid-50s, he had Type I diabetes and had to step down from active ministry. When he was still active, Phil had discovered the Camino de Santiago. He made it his life's passion.

Chapter 6

Phil explained that he had made 10 previous pilgrimage in sections along the Camino Francés. This was his 11th journey. He mentioned that he was only going about a week or so, as far as Logroño. Once there, he would have completed three complete transits of the Camino Francés.

We spent several hours chatting about the Camino, his ministry, English football, and various other issues. I found him a very interesting person to speak with. I asked if we might walk together the next day. He said yes, of course.

I was also invited to walk with other pilgrims by both Michelle and Vera, the two ladies I had helped earlier that day. At that point people began to look at me as someone who fixed stuff. That was fine with me.

I started this group dinner knowing maybe two or three people in the great room. By the time coffee was finished, after the rest of the dinner was consumed, I was known to some 30 or more pilgrims.

I am not by nature an extrovert. Indeed, most of my life I have been an introvert and a solitary person. But this was energizing. Here was a group of people united in one focused mission, to walk to Santiago de Compostela. Each person brought unique histories, backgrounds and skills to the journey. But by the end of the evening, we started thinking of ourselves as a family.

Here is a short anecdote that I am including for context, and amusement…

When I arrived at Refuge Orisson earlier that day, I was assigned a lower bunk in the room located under the café deck. I described this in an earlier story. However, after dinner, I returned to my bunk. I took in my laundry, now dried, repacked my rucksack for the next day and got ready for sleep, brushing teeth, taking medications, etc.

Other pilgrims assigned to sleep here started filing in, in

ones and twos. To my utter surprise, I discovered that I was sleeping with seven women that night! Seriously! There were eight beds arranged in four, double-high sets. I had one bottom bunk. If I recall correctly, I had seven female bunk mates from: South Africa, Japan, Ireland, Germany and Canada. Go figure.

Of course, this is silly. I only mention it because if I just said that one night on a Camino I slept with seven women, you just KNOW that people will get the wholly wrong idea.

Suffice it to say the snorers snored, the belchers belched, and we were all too tired to mind much. Besides, I had gotten the memo about bringing earplugs and an eyeshade. I had both. I do not know what the others had, because I could neither see nor hear them. I snuggled into my SnugPak "Traveller" sleeping bag for the night https://snugpakusa.com/product.php?id=12

It was a good thing I went with this sleeping bag because one of my colleagues decided that she needed the door open to the outside for fresh air.

I suppose that the takeaway from this experience was that we are all adults and pilgrims. We share the same objectives and respected each other. That is all that mattered.

All in all, it was a successful first day on a first Camino. I was looking forward to the coming days and weeks.

7

Whee! This Reminds Me of Being a Wee Lass

Crossing the Pyrenees

April 2013 (P)

My second morning on the Camino Francés started early leaving Refuge Orisson so early that the sun was not fully up and the temperature was in the low single digits Celsius. But as I was to come to learn, Santiago is not coming to you. If you want to see him, you have to put one foot in front of the other and get there. I put on layers of clothing and just pushed off.

I and my straggling Camino Family from the previous evening all started out in the wintry cold. Apparently, southern France and the Pyrenees region were considered to be having a late winter that year. This was seen in the several inches of snow we encountered after leaving the paved road to turn towards the Spanish frontier. The snow was ankle deep in places.

While it was clear and sunny, it was quite cold. I had a baseball style cap and a bucket style sun hat. I was warm, but my ears were frozen. I had used an old winter survival tip I knew and was wearing an extra pair of merino wool socks on my hands as mittens. But, this did nothing for my ears. This is when it dawned on me that everything you bring on Camino should have at least two purposes to be worth carrying. Socks as mittens, check…

As we are walking along, the group that had left Refuge

Orisson started stringing out according to walking speeds, styles and fitness levels. We crossed the frontier and encountered Roland's Fountain said to be there, since a famous battle fought so many centuries ago. While being referred to as the Napoleón Pass, with attribution stemming from the Peninsular War between England, France and Spain in the early 1800s, this route was actually the primary route over the Pyrenees for most pilgrims to Santiago coming from northern and central Europe.

Many very old pilgrim routes from all over northern and central Europe converged at Le Puy, Toulouse, and then Saint Jean Pied de Port, France, enroute to one of the most popular mountain passes used to cross over the Pyrenees Mountains. Other passes to the east and west handled pilgrims coming from the Atlantic coast and from southeastern France and Italy.

After the fountain and walking over one of the innumerable cattle grates installed on the path to keep livestock on one side or the other, we came upon a wooded area on the north side of a mountain where the path was relatively flat. To either side of the path, going up the mountain to the upper tree line, and below the path as far as the eye could see, were forests of birch trees. When these trees shed their leaves in the autumn, the leaves accumulated on the path.

As we walked along the path, our feet fell ankle deep in the accumulated dropped leaves. In the woods, to either side of the path was snow that could not melt as it was mostly in the shade.

I am walking along, when I hear a swishing sound coming from behind me and advancing fast. As I turned to see what the sound was I hear my new friend Vera, the lady of the Hello Kitty lost iPhone, crying gleefully at the top of her voice: "Whee, this reminds me of being a wee lass!" Here we are walking on the Camino Francés and this woman is literally skipping, not running or walking, but skipping, as she cries out in joy.

Chapter 7

It could not but make me start laughing out loud, as did others in the immediate area. We were amused at her sheer joy of kicking the birch leaves into the air with abandon, presumably as she did as a young child in Ireland. Vera appeared to be having the time of her life.

After about five minutes she caught up and we walked together for some distance as she explained this joyful moment. It was pretty much as I explained it.

Vera told me that, as a child growing up in Ireland, she loved to walk on "Birch Walks." These were paths like this one, where the fallen birch leaves accumulated. I had never heard of this. I was also not one to kick leaves into the air as in my life, I was the fellow who had to rake them into piles each autumn.

In the conversation, Vera mentioned how cold her ears were and that she had forgotten to bring a hat. To help, I gave her my ballcap, explaining that I had a second hat, whereas I only had one head.

Little did I know at that moment that this simple act was a preview of a significant part of the rest of my first Camino. I did not realize it then, but three days later, at Pamplona, I would hit on a major idea.

8

Can You Fix It – Redux?
Roncesvalles, Navarra, Spain

April 2013 (P)

After four or five hours of walking from France into Spain, then taking the alternative road route down from the mountain pass to Roncesvalles, I finally arrived at the former monastery. That monastery is presently the albergue where arriving pilgrims usually stay overnight, having just walked from Saint Jean Pied de Port in one day, or split into two, as I had done.

This albergue is very large, offering something like 180 beds nightly, all in very modern well-maintained facilities. It is operated on behalf of the local government and church by volunteers from the Netherlands Genootschap Van Sint Jacob. This is the Dutch friends of Saint James organization. This albergue is spotless, very well managed, and has very strict rules.

On arrival, I received my stamp (sello) in my pilgrim credencial, paid my fee, and was assigned to a bed. I found the lower bunk bed as directed and was shocked at how nice it all was. There was even a locked closet for my rucksack with a key that operated by putting one Euro in a slot. The coin was returned every time you opened the locker using the key.

I got settled in. One of the things I had read was that you should open and lay out your sleeping bag or liner to demonstrate that the bed was taken, that no one should presume it was empty and could be taken, and I did this.

As I opened up my new – used one night – Snug Pak sleeping bag, a zipper slider came off in my hand. On closer examination, it appeared the very fine, taffeta-like fabric used for this very lightweight sleeping bag had caught in the slider and zipper teeth, allowing the zipper to be wedged up and off the zipper proper.

This definitely was not a good thing. Here I was only on the second night of a planned 35 to 40-day journey across northwestern Spain, with a later than normal winter. Oh, and by the way, some of the other pilgrims traveling with me decided that even though heat was provided in the albergue, they preferred sleeping with the windows wide open. I knew I would need to get that zipper slider back on track, so to speak.

I tried to work with it to try to wedge it back onto the zipper track. But my skills fell seriously short of what was needed. At this point I decided that what I needed to do was to shower, do my wash, and find some beer.

After bathing and changing into clean clothing for the next day, I went downstairs where they had pay-go service to have volunteers do your laundry for a set price using washing machines and driers. The laundry would be washed, dried and folded for you to pick up later. WOW! I had the thought that if all albergues were like this, my pilgrimage might even be fun… hah!

After leaving my laundry off, I set out for food. I managed to find a meal at a family-style table in a local restaurant. They offered a fixed price pilgrim meal. I sat at a table with perhaps seven or eight others, most from my informal pilgrim family. But fate had a surprise for me.

Previously, I introduced a woman named Michelle who

was walking the Camino de Santiago as a tribute to her late husband. You might recall how I mentioned in that story how her youthful passion was to become a seamstress but that her parents insisted she get a proper job. As mentioned, she worked her entire career in nursing.

Well, I had seen her loping far ahead of me on the path earlier in the day. Although she was less than five feet tall, she had the hiking pace of a speed walker. She was not speed walking mind you, Michelle just had the sure footedness and pace of a gazelle – poof – she was gone. Yet, there she was sitting opposite me at the round table.

Over dinner, I asked her about her seamstress skills and if she had sewing materials with her. She indicated she always traveled with repair supplies as other hikers always seemed attracted to her seamstress skills. Ah HA! Success! I explained the predicament I had with my sleeping bag. Michelle said she would be happy to see what could be done.

After dinner, dessert, and a few more beers, we went back to the albergue, I brought my sleeping bag downstairs so Michelle could examine it. I was already forming a Plan B in my mind, where I would use safety pins to partially close the open side of the sleeping bag, then replace it once I got to Pamplona. I had no idea where I might do this, but I figured Pamplona should have an outdoors store where I might buy a suitable sleeping bag.

Michelle came with her sewing kit. I use the term loosely because what she had was an abbreviated version of what a tailor might have in their shop. Everything was arranged in a fold up – roll up fly fishing lure case. It was truly ingenious. I love clever gadgets; this was amazing.

She examined the sleeping bag zipper. I gave her the sliders from my sleeping bag. There were actually two sliders originally installed. The idea was that you could arrange the two sliders to have an open portion at the bottom of the bag while closing the top, or vice versa.

Anyway, after examining everything she announced, Yup, I can do this. But to make it work, you can only have one slider going in one direction (up or down) and I have to secure the bottom end of the zipper track tape to make it work.

Once I asked, and was reassured that this would work, I asked her to do it. She told me that I had to be extra careful to prevent the taffeta nylon fabric from clogging the zipper pull again.

Long story short, and here, I think is the moral of the story. What goes around comes around. Karma has a way of catching up with you…

The previous day, I had fixed Michelle's broken hiking pole at Orisson. It worked fine all that day walking over the Pyrenees. She continued to be very pleased that she could continue to use her late husband's hiking poles.

Now, she had saved me from freezing while I slept in a large bunk room shared with maybe 60 other pilgrims, too many of who were determined to sleep with windows wide open. I seriously needed that sleeping bag to close properly, and close it did.

I had a restful night, froze when I had to get out of the bag to use the toilet or to shower. I was actually happy to be thrown out by the volunteers who came through at 7:30 am rousting everyone out before 8:00 am. The loud classical music had started at 7:00, just in case you forgot to set an alarm…

9

Walking Pneumonia

Pamplona, Navarra, Spain

April 2013 (P)

Earlier, I mentioned that the weather was unusually cold in the last week of April even with bright sunny days. Well, the day we left the large Roncesvalles albergue, it started to rain. Now, it was totally overcast, cold, wet, and raw. Everyone had to wear their rain gear, and most had soaked lower legs where our ponchos and raincoats ended. I was no different.

A large part of the days' walking was along roads, walking on macadam paved surfaces, or through small villages on wet sidewalks or paved paths.

The third night of my first Camino was spent at the municipal albergue in Larrasoaña. Only six euros, another sello for my credencial, and I was assigned to a lower bunk. As the clothes washing tubs were outside, uncovered and being rained on, there would be no washing and drying on a line outdoors. I had to do my hand wash in the bathroom sink after I showered.

From there things got interesting. Although I had wrung out my washed clothes as well as I could, finding a place to hang the clothing to dry was a challenge. In the end I managed to make a field-expedient clothesline under the frame of the upper bunk, over my lower bunk. Everything got hung.

The problem was that the humidity was so high in this albergue that there was literally condensation on the walls.

The rooms smelled musty. I would later learn that there was nil heat in the building at night. The building was damp, cold, and musty. All the heat available insofar as I could tell was coming from the other seven men in the other double-tiered bunks in this one room.

After having a meal in a local bar / café, I returned to my damp clothes hung around my damp bunk. I slept warm, but damp in my sleeping bag. Fortunately, the bag's insulation was synthetic and not down. I managed to sleep. Not a good night's sleep, as I started feeling ill. But I slept.

The following morning, the weather was a repeat of the previous day, overcast, raining and raw. None of my clothes were dry from the previous afternoon. But it was necessary to press on to reach Pamplona.

Early during the day, I started coughing and having chest congestion. By late morning, I felt as though I was running a fever. But there was nothing for it but to press on.

By mid-afternoon, and approaching Pamplona, I was feeling really ill. My chest was very congested and I was coughing up very colorful phlegm. I resolved to go to the first farmacia I came to on arrival in Pamplona.

At Pamplona, I went into a farmacia on the Plaza Major. Fortunately, the pharmacist spoke fairly good English. I conveyed my symptoms. He actually produced a single-use thermometer and took my temperature. This confirmed that I did in fact have a higher-than-normal temperature and his considered opinion was that I likely had a serious case of bronchitis, sometimes called walking pneumonia.

I asked for some cough syrup to address the cough and chest congestion, as well as the sore throat that I was having. Also, I was experiencing intermittent chills. The pharmacist understood I was on the Camino and staying in albergues. He strongly recommended that I consider staying in a hotel where I could medicate and get warm.

As I had no idea how to find a hotel. I asked if he could direct me to the nearest tourist information office. He and his mother, who were both working, were very kind and drew me a map to get to the TI (Oficina de Tourisms).

Only about four short city blocks away, the TI had an English-speaking staff. At this point, my Spanish was limited to phrase books and the Google Translate app on my iPod Touch, when I had Wi-Fi internet access.

Approaching the counter, I explained to the young lady that I was a pilgrim, was ill, and needed a hotel room to nurse myself back to health. She had just served another English-speaking pilgrim I will call Janet. Janet commented to me that she just got a recommendation for a nearby hotel that was family run, inexpensive and well regarded. That was enough for me. I asked Janet if she minded if we walked over together. The TI staff called the hotel to tell them we were both coming over and needed two rooms.

Together, off to the Hotel Eslava we went. Just off the Camino path on the way out of the old town, we arrived and were assigned to separate rooms. We agreed to meet for breakfast the next day before starting out.

After checking in, I showered, did my hand wash, turned the heat up, and used my hiking pole to hang my hand wash over the radiator that provided blessed heat. As the room came with linens, I was able to roll and stomp my wrung out washed clothes in a bath towel to remove almost all the water. This was a trick I had learned years ago, and it held me in good stead now. I also re-washed the clothes that I had tried to wash at Larrasoaña but which were still wet.

Before I left the hotel to find something to eat, I took pain relievers and some of the cough medicine from the farmacia. I recall that I ended up having pizza, and walked around the old town for a few hours.

After playing tourist for a few hours and with darkness coming, I returned to the Hotel to have an early night. That night I luxuriated in a private room with a private bathroom and HEAT!

Before going to sleep, I took a double dose of the cough syrup medication from the farmacia, some pain relievers to address both my fever and my aches and pains, and got under the bed covers in my sleeping bag. That night I sweated out my nasty bronchitis. I know it sounds odd, but it evidently worked. The next morning, I felt 100 percent better. Not completely well, but well enough to continue.

My First Ever China Store!
Pamplona, Navarra, Spain

April 2013 (P)

As I just mentioned, I had only a few hours to wander about the old town of Pamplona. I felt like death warmed over, and I needed to eat and get back to my hotel to nurse myself in the hope that I would be able to continue on my Camino the next day.

As I was wandering up and down the narrow old streets, I stumbled upon an odd-looking shop that was called Asia Bazar, if I remember correctly. From the outside it looked like a variety store, but had no theme per se. Being curious I walked in. WOW! This place was like a container ship coming from mainland China had exploded, and all the wide variety of inexpensive items had found their way here.

Trying to describe the scope of what these products were would take many pages. Suffice it to say that the shop had a little bit of everything from kitchen goods, to cooking, storage, pet items, electrical items, tools, stationery items, clothing, travel accessories, and more, and more still…

I looked for and found a very inexpensive pair of microfiber gloves as I had been freezing for three days and using spare merino wool socks as mittens. Then I stumbled on something that would have a profound effect on the rest of my Camino.

There was literally a stack of black, microfleece tubular

sleeves with a toggle closure on top. According to the very funny printed material attached to the item, it could be worn about seven different ways. I say funny because on one side of the label it had photos of an Asian woman depicting the various ways to wear the garment. On the opposite side was a Western woman wearing the same garment in exactly the same manner, with no variation. I thought the cultural disconnect was hilarious. Like, why would anyone wear the item differently, East to West?

Among other approaches, it could be worn as a neck cover, a headband, a balaclava, and most importantly a beanie / watch cap if you pulled the toggle closure closed. I tried one on in the store and determined that it solved my frozen ear problem and would make an excellent hat for the cold and raw weather I was experiencing. Also, I knew that being microfleece, it was lightweight and would insulate even when wet. One of these potentially very useful clothing items only cost Euro 1,20. I bought twelve of them.

I had experienced a "lightbulb moment." Several days earlier I had given away a ballcap to a woman with no hat. But I needed this new beanie to keep my head warm. But it occurred to me that I could hand them out to others who might have similarly been caught up by the late winter. Ah HA!

I literally had to put my hands in my pockets to prevent myself from buying dozens of items. There were so many clever and inexpensive items that I had never seen before anywhere. One example where I did break down and spend more was a package of silicon rubber bands. They were conventionally sized but superior to a standard rubber bands. Moreover, they were in several neon-like dayglo colors. Seven years later, I am still using them.

I was later to discover that these stores exist in most every large Spanish town and city, the larger places have multiple shops. The names vary, but are usually similar to Asia Bazar, China Bazar, Oriental Bazar, etc. In the years since and in many places, I have found these shops to be excellent places to find little clever items that helped me get thought a Camino, fix broken stuff, or just make life on a Camino more convenient. I recommend them highly.

11

Sky Diving – With No Parachute
Alto de Perdón, Navarra, Spain

May 2013 (P)

It was still overcast and threatening rain when Janet and I left our hotel in Pamplona the next morning. I managed to sweat out my bronchial illness overnight. While not operating at full healthy capacity, I felt well enough to move on down the road.

The old section of Pamplona ends near the hotel, where there is a green belt of parks that surround the oldest part of town. Most of the walk to leave Pamplona was on city streets until we got to more residential areas and eventually farm sendas, or maintained farm trails with a sand and gravel texture to walk on.

The day's destination was Puente La Reina (Bridge of the Queen). Before arriving here, one had to walk up Alto del Perdón. While not overly high at about 790 meters, it is nonetheless still a rather high hill to climb. It is also the first hill of any size since coming over the Pyrenees.

Walking through farmland to approach this hill, one sees a wind farm of a dozen or more high-tech wind generators along the ridge line in the distance. This was to become a frequent sight all along the Camino. If there was a mountain ridge with a regular wind, you could bet on seeing these wind turbines. They are HUGE when you get right up to them.

Approaching the hill up to Alto del Perdón, the slope

gradually increases. To the right side is pasture land. To the left, is scrub brush extending up the hill. The actual path is perhaps two meters wide, just barely wide enough for two people to walk abreast. However, we experienced a fair number of bicycle pilgrims, and being near to Pamplona, a fair number day tripper bike riders, all clad in their finest lycra and spandex. This meant that we walking pilgrims necessarily defaulted to walking single-file much of the time.

As we continued to ascend the hill, the rain increased and each of us put on our raingear cinching our hoods about our heads. This had the effect of reducing forward vision to a limited and narrow view. The rain was never hard, just constant, a heavy drizzle.

Ascending the hill, I noticed that the slope to the right was becoming more and more steep the higher we got. Conversely, the upward slope to the left of the trail, was more or less constant. About 200 meters before the top of the hill, the right slope transitioned into a near sheer, very steep drop off. It did occur to me that falling from this height would be a death sentence as people wearing backpacks typically broke their necks when falling down a severe slope.

I mentioned previously that it was raining and we all had our rain coat or poncho hoods cinched tight to keep rain out. We were walking single-file and Janet, the woman I had met in the tourism information office the previous day, was walking point as the first person in our tiny group or string of pilgrims.

Here I am, minding my own business, enjoying the ambiance and the very nice views, following the person in front of me using my hiking poles to help gain traction in the now muddy soil, when all of a sudden, I hear a very loud scream in English - "WATCH OUT!" Military training from decades earlier kicked in and I dove off the trail to the right. Janet, who first saw the approaching threat leaped to the left, of course!

Did I forget to mention that, for those who jumped off the trail to the right, there was no there, there? I did mention that some 200 meters before the summit of Alto del Perdón the slope on the right dropped off into a near vertical slope.

Well, in one split second, I realized that oh %^&*, there is nothing but air there! I dug my right hiking pole into the ground and watched as it bowed into an archery bow shape. I tried to get low to the ground to not be top-heavy.

The next thing I remember is being on my left knee, with my right leg dangling over the edge, and I was vomiting up my very good breakfast from the hotel in Pamplona. It took a moment or two for my vision to clear up. I was likely reviewing my entire life flashing before me just second before. I retrieved my hiking pole, noticing that it had returned to straight, from being bowed severely.

Janet came and helped me up. All I could do, shaking like a leaf, was to ask her what just happened. All she could tell me at that point was that two spandex clad cyclists came barreling down the trail forcing walking pilgrims to leap off the trail. They sounded no bell, horn or verbal alert. Now, I felt light-headed and mildly nauseous. Realizing I had just dodged death, I suggested we proceed the rest of the way to the top of Alto del Perdón.

At the top there is a small surprise for those of you who have seen the film *The Way*. The bronze sculptures on the top of a hill in the film are actually at the top of Alto del Perdón. They make a nice backdrop for photos.

Once you are at this scenic overlook, the rest of the trip into Puente La Reina is downhill. This is considered one of the more treacherous downhill segments on the Camino Francés as it has a lot of loose rocks of small size that can make getting a good footing difficult.

After arriving at my hotel in Puente La Reina and settling in, I joined several of the other pilgrims for a glass or three of wine. I had quite the exciting day.

Chatting with two men from Ireland, Janet came over to join us. I was relating my recollection of the day's excitement. As she heard my version, she added that I did not know the half of it. I asked her what she meant. She told me that I only knew part of the story. Here is the full story as Janet reconstructed it and shared it with us:

- The walk up the hill, single file, with cinched-down rain gear was as I recalled it above.

- Janet's alert was as I stated. But she was able to add that these two fellows had driven their bicycles to the top of Alto de Perdón on top of a car, to have a 'wicked good' and fast ride to the bottom of the hill.

- As I recalled, there was no early alert (bell, horn, whistle, or voice) to their overtaking us head-on. Janet saw them come around a turn in the trail, very fast, instantly recognized the threat, and screamed at the top of her lungs to alert everyone behind her. She jumped into the brush and bushes to the left.

- The first spandex clad rider just blew right by perhaps half a dozen of us without uttering a word.

- The second rider apparently saw me headed for a long sky-dive without a parachute. He managed to dump his bicycle in the brush to his right, and reach out with his left hand to grab my left side rucksack strap a moment before I went over the edge of the mountain.

- This was the very same moment that I watched my hiking pole bend like an archery bow and dropped to one knee.

- The second rider grabbed his bike and continued down the hill as soon as he realized I was not going over the edge.

I never saw nor spoke to either of these bicycle riders. But the second fellow actually saved my life. That is when I asked for another bottle of vino tinto…

Aftermath and Update:

Hiking Poles –

On returning home in June, I e-mailed Leki in the Czech Republic to thank them for making a hiking pole that literally saved my life. It was a product testimonial. Imagine my surprise, when about a month later, a parcel arrived in the mail with a new set of Leki hiking poles, from the Czech Republic. Okay, I am sold. Good customer service will win me over every time.

While I have transitioned to very lightweight carbon fiber hiking poles made by Black Diamond in recent years, I still have that set of lifesaving Leki Ultra Lightweight aluminum hiking poles. Let's just say that I am attached to them. I use them for all my local training hikes.

The free replacement poles were donated to my local chapter of the American Pilgrims on the Camino (APOC). I did not need three sets of poles.

Safety On The Trail –

As from 2014, the next year, there is now a thick sturdy safety cable with steel poles set into the right edge of the steep section of this trail ascending Alto del Perdón. It is still possible to catch this cable at about knee height and fall over the edge, but at least you would have something secure to grab onto to prevent what almost happened to me in 2013.

12

Got Caps?
Camino Francés, Spain

May 2013 (P)

Earlier, I wrote about my first ever China store or Asian Bazar in Pamplona. I also mentioned that I obtained a dozen very inexpensive but potentially very useful microfleece tubes that could be worn as warm hats. I was already wearing mine, at least in the early morning.

After my near-death experience at Alto del Perdón the previous day coming up the hill, and the follow-up debriefing by my pilgrim colleague Janet that evening, I decided to start giving away the eleven extra caps to pilgrims I met along the way who needed one. Having been saved by a random act of kindness, I felt compelled to repay the kindness somehow. It occurred to me that simply giving away the inexpensive but very effective microfleece caps was exactly the sort of thing that would meet the need.

No matter that the fellow who likely saved my life was the proximate cause of my almost losing it. He and I were placed there at that moment for a reason. A very deep philosophical lesson was learned. It would be one of the first I would learn over several Caminos and multiple years.

Also, being out of doors in wintry weather causes you to lose most of your body heat through your head and ears. If you can keep these bits covered and warm, you save a lot of energy and preserve body heat.

I recall the first hat I gave away was to Vera. You may recall that she was the older Irish lady who lost and recovered her Hello Kitty clad iPhone on the first day out of Saint Jean Pied de Port, and who I gave my ballcap to on the second day of our journey to Santiago.

Well, on the way out of Puente La Reina, or more accurately, at breakfast, I encountered her again. She remarked that she really liked the look of my new microfleece beanie. Vera did not have anything more than the ballcap I had given her three days earlier, so I gave her one. When Vera offered to pay, I just told her to just pay it forward, and do something for another pilgrim in need.

To make it easy to get at my stash of microfleece caps, I stored them in an outside mesh stretchy pocket on my rucksack. This way, I could ask another pilgrim to pull out the white plastic shopping bag, remove one cap and stuff the remainder back in the mesh pocket.

Over the coming several weeks, I was to give away all my caps. Plus, when the supply was depleted later, at Ponferrada I scored another success when I bought ten more caps in yet another Asia Bazar shop. I would have bought more, but that was all they had. The cost was still only Euro 1,20 each. I continued to hand out these caps all along the remainder of the Camino Francés until just after starting the final segment from Sarria.

You might wonder why I am including this particular story, and why here, when it spans most all of my first Camino in April – May 2013. Well, there are two reasons.

First, it demonstrated aptly the concept of helping others in need, without being asked. If I encountered any pilgrim who appeared to have inadequate headgear for the late winter we were experiencing, I could partially remedy that condition. In addition, it offered the opportunity to explain to others how they could use an extra pair of socks as mittens until they could obtain gloves for their cold hands.

Second, the process of handing out the hats was to have a profound effect on me later on. It is also featured in part in at least two other stories in this book. As a result, it is necessary to insert this story somewhere around the time the entire thing got started to properly set the stage for what follows. Be patient. Telling the entire story here would affect other humorous or interesting stories if I relate too much out of context and proper chronology.

Suffice it to say for now, that after Pamplona I started giving away warm microfleece hats to pilgrims who got caught out by the later winter and needed better head gear. I just happened to think of it there and then. Almost flying off Alto del Perdón also nudged me into action. I admit that much.

By this point in my first Camino, less than a week out from Saint Jean Pied de Port, I was already starting to feel that there was a dimension to this whole pilgrimage thing what was new and arguably alien to me. This activity was, in part, my way of trying to experience and learn more about exactly what the heck was happening.

Walking in the Steps of
Francis of Assisi
Puente la Reina, Navarra, Spain

April 2013 (P)

Leaving the town of Puenta la Reina, one encounters some significant bits of Spanish history. The original name of the town was Puente de Argo, as the bridge just after the city spanned the River Argo.

The bridge itself was replaced during the 12th Century to better support the larger numbers of pilgrims traveling onward to Santiago via this route. In the process, Queen Muniadona, wife of King Sancho III, caused the change in the bridge name. Instead of just being the bridge of the river Argo, it became the Queen's Bridge, after the project sponsor or instigator.

Moreover, the town proper was the first town after the confluence of another Camino route. The Camino Aragonés flows into the Camino Francés at or just before Puenta la Reina. This route conveyed pilgrims from southeastern France, and the Provence Region, over the Pyrenees at the Somport Pass. It is this happenstance that leads to the title of this short story.

In the year 1213, Francis of Assisi departed Assisi to make pilgrimage to venerate the relics of the Apostle Saint James (Santiago) at Santiago de Compostela. He was accompanied by two of his followers. Consider that at that time if you wanted to get from point A to point B you walked unless you had a horse or other animal to ride or to pull your carriage or cart.

Francis being, well Francis, walked. We know he wore his long tunic robe with hood, had simple sandals, carried a staff and likely a gourd to hold water. That is about all we know or can infer from historical information.

We know that he walked north through the Italian peninsula, along the Cinque Terra, the Italian Riviera, into the French kingdoms, along the French Riviera, Provence, and eventually crossed the Pyrenees at the Somport Pass, crossing into the then Kingdom of Aragón. Historically, this is the same source location for Katherine of Aragón, who would centuries later be one of King Henry VIII of England's wives.

From the Somport Pass, we know that Francis and his followers journeyed on what is now the Camino Aragonés, eventually winding up at Puenta la Reina. This is where any contemporary Camino journey starts to get very interesting from an historical and religious standpoint.

We know from historical records that Francis and his followers continued on to Santiago, visiting several Franciscan groups and churches along the way. The most significant of these was likely the Franciscan church at O'Cebreiro. This church, founded by Francis of Assisi, exists and operates to this day.

He arrived in Santiago in 1214. After a stay of some duration, and with a new tunic and sandals provided by his Santiago Franciscan followers, he turned around and walked back to Italy. He arrived back at Assisi sometime in 1215.

As one departs the really old walls of Puente la Reina, and before the bridge out of town, you pass through an ancient gate in the walls surrounding the town that has been there for more than a thousand years. Francis of Assisi and his two followers would have had to walk through this same narrow gate to leave Puenta la Reina.

Stop and think about that for a moment. This holy man walked on the exact pavement and may have touched the same side lintels to this rather narrow stone gate. As I recall, it was sized as narrow as it was so a mounted rider on a horse seeking to invade the town could not enter through this gate. I clearly recall having to walk single-file through the stone gate.

Now, past the protective medieval walls of the town, you can see the Romanesque styled bridge. At times it has also been called the Puente Romántica. It is a rather attractive bridge. When built, it was wide enough for carts to come and go, as well as to support large numbers of pilgrims.

In 2013, when I walked this route, just beyond the bridge pilgrims encountered the remnants of the original Roman road. The road had not been upgraded, filled in with sand or fine gravel to make it easier to walk on. The surface consisted of well weathered and rounded stones with gaps in between as well as ruts worn by centuries of cart wheel.

The thing that hit me square in the brain as I was stepping over these somewhat uneven stones was that these were likely the exact stones that Francis of Assisi walked on some 800 years earlier. Now, THAT gave me chicken skin, or goose bumps!

I did not set out to do the Camino de Santiago as a religious pilgrimage. In fact, that first night at Orisson, when all the others in the dining room were explaining their motivations for doing the Camino, when they got around to me, I stated that I was doing the Camino for "all of the above reasons."

Okay, so I happen to be a Cradle Catholic. That means that I was born into the faith. My earliest education was in a Franciscan run school and church parish. As a result, any association between Saint Francis of Assisi and the Camino affects me as I have a special affinity for this particular Catholic saint.

But this, walking on the same stones he walked on, to me

was something akin to walking the Via Dolorosa in Jerusalem. I well understand the theological differences. But it resonated with me then and continues to this day.

I was told, but cannot confirm that since 2013 someone decided to make the path easier for pilgrims by improving the surface of that original Roman road just after the Puente la Reina bridge. My information was that the road was filled in and at least leveled. I do not have confirmation one way or the other.

But, even if the original road has been buried under cinders, fine gravel or sand to level the walking surface, I hope they left the original Roman road there as a sub-surface. I really do.

14

Filming Jesus, With Rev. Phil
After Puente La Reina

April 2013 (P)

As mentioned in an earlier chapter, I met my Camino Family the first night out of Saint Jean Pied de Port, at Refuge Orisson. I just happened to wind up sitting across the table from a bearded fellow who I started chatting with. This was the entire purpose of the large family style dinner. We interacted with one another forming our informal Camino family for the next month or so.

We introduced ourselves, beyond the already baselined first name, where one was from and why we were doing the Camino. My new acquaintance was named Phil Wren. It took several additional days of intermittently walking together for me to piece together his back story.

I am not by nature nosy, nor do I asking prying or searching questions. I had to do that during my career, and frankly, I was tired of knowing more than I needed to know. If people wanted to volunteer information that was fine by me, but my days of interrogating folks was long over.

In one of the more prying questions, I did ask if Phil might not be related to the famous architect of Saint Paul's Cathedral in London, Sir Christopher Wren. I had never met anyone with the family name Wren. To me at least, it seemed a reasonable question. Phil explained that he was indeed a distant relation to the famous architect. Go figure! What a small world.

By the time we ambled over the Pyrenees to Roncesvalles, Pamplona, and then to Puente la Reina, I had determined that Phil was actually the Reverend Philip J. Wren, a Methodist minister formerly from a parish near Liverpool, England. Phil loved football (soccer) and was a rabid Manchester United fan. He had a loving and very patient wife as well as grown children. Over that first meal, we chatted about this and that.

Phil tried to drag me into political discussions. Having traveled extensively all over the world, over several decades, I had learned to avoid these sort of discussions whenever possible. My experience is that many folks do not meet that many Americans in person, such as this setting. As a result, we tend to serve as a sort of a lightning rod for all the accumulated frustration, anger, or whatever adverse emotion one felt at that moment. Some of these feelings may have developed over years. Ergo, I prudently, I think, changed the subject to careers.

That is how I learned that Phil had type-one diabetes. Because of this and related ailments, he was compelled to retire from active ministry in his mid-50s. His passion in retirement was the Camino.

He explained to me that prior to this trip he had walked ten segments of the Camino Francés. His statement to me was that he was only going as far as Logroño this time. Once he reached that small city, he would have completed three complete Camino Francés pilgrimages, over eleven segments. He planned to take a bus to the coast, then a ferry "back to Blighty" to use his exact words.

Moreover, Phil was a speaker associated with the Confraternity of Saint James (CSJ) speaker's bureau in London. When a group or organization desired a presentation or lecture about the Camino, Phil was among the featured speakers assigned to that purpose.

To that end, Phil carried a high-end video and still digital camera. He was intent on gathering additional still and video footage to improve his presentations when speaking to groups. His pilgrim walking staff was actually a camera monopod. To see Phil all kitted out in his typical pilgrim regalia was hysterical. What a character!

In addition to wearing a medium length beard, Phil wore a traditional brown felt pilgrim hat with the front brim turned up and a scallop shell pin holding the brim in place.

Because of circulatory issues, Phil wore sport hiking sandals, even in the snow. He also wore a bright, international orange poncho. I still have a cherished photo of Phil on the birch walk just after we crossed into Spain. This path was discussed in the context of Vera's kicking the fallen birch leaves into the air with childlike glee.

After leaving Puenta la Reina, Phil and I found ourselves walking together more. As we started to come out of the mountains, we began to enter rolling farmlands. This was the end of April, and some fields were already blooming.

There were abundant wild flowers, especially red poppies. Frequently, Phil would stop to take a photo of something, anything really. Occasionally, he would attach the digital camera to the monopod and capture video.

Usually, and especially when he was trying to video something, I would hold his cape the really bright orange poncho, out of the way so the wind would not blow it into the camera's view, or the wind would not cause the poncho to snap, making noises not needed on the video.

One such sunny day, we came across a farm with fields on both sides of the path that had apparently been planted in some variety of winter wheat. The wheat stalks were perhaps four to five feet tall (about 1.5 meters). In the more or less constant wind, the wheat moved to and fro. There was actually a sound to it.

Phil stopped, cocked his head and exclaimed, "Do you hear that?" My reply was "What?" He persisted, telling me he HAD to capture this phenomenon. He mounted the camera to set up for capturing the rhythmic swaying of the wheat, as well as the sound it made.

At this point, I am sort of humoring Phil. As I had been doing as his errant squire, I held his poncho out of the way, and anything else he could not handle while filming.

He got set up and started filming the swaying wheat and we both become absolutely silent. After some 30 seconds or so, with me silently fidgeting, Phil turned to me and softly said. "Do you HEAR IT?" I replied as before, but I did allow that I did hear a very soft silent swishing sound.

Phil turned, looking right through me, and said quite plainly that THAT was the sound of God in nature. It was to him as plain as the nose on his face, and he desperately wanted others to hear it. Phil was positively thrilled to have captured it on video. He was genuinely excited by having captured the sight and sound on video knowing that it would become a highlight of his future Camino lectures and presentations.

I allowed that I knew I heard something although I had not the experience he had, interpreting the Divine. After all, who am I to question a man of God?

15

The Pilgrim Who Did Not Wake Up?
Logroño, Rioja, Spain

May 2013 (P)

After several more days of the typical pilgrim daily pattern: rise, walk, eat, walk, stop, bathe, do your hand wash, hang it to dry, eat, drink, sleep, wake and repeat, until you arrive at Santiago de Compostela, we arrived at the small city of Logroño. Here I had made a hotel reservation having learned the previously week that staying in albergues did not agree with my health.

As Phil and I walked into the city we came to the municipal albergue. I still had three or four more city blocks to go to get to my night's lodging. We were exchanging pleasantries and preparing to part ways. I specifically recall Phil commenting that: "My journey has come to an end – this is where my Camino ends." Those were Phil's exact words and I recall them clearly to this day.

We wished one another a Buen Camino, shook hands and even had a man hug. I turned away and went to my hotel lodgings.

The next morning was 1 May. I had breakfast and departed my lodgings headed west towards Burgos. It would be several days before I reached that historic and very interesting city.

After taking two rest days at Burgos to deal with a medical issue on one of my feet (this is discussed later in a related story about needing a pedicure), I stopped at a café for coffee following my exit from the city. By this time, my original Camino family was spread all over the place, and I had not seen any of them for a about a week. But, as I was sharing a table with others, enjoying my mid-morning coffee and tortilla snack, I overheard several Canadian pilgrims discussing a pilgrim who had died in his sleep.

With some trepidation, I introduced myself to them and the conversation. In doing this, I learned that a pilgrim had gone to sleep in the Logroño municipal albergue and had been found deceased the following morning. Now, my seriously obsessive and analytical brain clicked into high gear, and the questions came out:

- Exactly when did this happen – the night of April 30 into 1 May.

- Who found this situation? – When everyone awoke the next morning, this pilgrim did not move. A German pilgrim couple determined he was not responsive and began CPR. Albergue staff called the ambulance.

- Do you know the name of the pilgrim? (No) Nationality? (No)

- Were you staying at that same albergue? (Yes)

- Can you describe the pilgrim? (Sort of…)

- Did he wear a beard? (Yes)

- Did he have a bright orange poncho? (Yes)

- Did he have an expensive camera? (I think so)

They followed by stating that the ambulance crew removed the body.

Now, my brain is in overdrive. My intellect tells me that, for many objective reasons, this could well be Phil. Everything fit the facts I knew. But I had no way to confirm this story. The only link I had was the popular Camino Forum run by a Norwegian expat living in Santiago de Compostela.

In those years I did not have a smartphone, only an iPod touch, and I needed free Wi-Fi at a hotel or café. The next opportunity I had, later that day, I fired off a message to the fellow who runs the forum to ask if they knew anything. I shared the questions and answers I mentioned above. The immediate answer was no, but they would watch out. From that point onwards, I continued to make inquires when I could.

Sometime later, at Astorga, I stayed in the Hotel Gaudí and had a beer on the terrace, sharing a table with a young lady who happened to be on the British Embassy staff at Madrid. I explained everything I knew and told her that, being a retired civil servant myself, I well understood that she could not discuss personal issues like this. All I asked for was a yes or no, and asked her if she would not mind checking in with the consular section then just providing confirmation. I gave her both my e-mail and mobile flip phone numbers. I never heard from her.

A day or so later, when I arrived at Rabanal, I stopped in at the excellent CSJ-run albergue Gaucelmo to make inquiries. As luck would have it, I missed the previous UK-based volunteer crew by only 30 minutes. The new group of volunteers were from Orlando, Florida, and did not know anything.

It was not until several days later that news finally hit the Camino Forum. It was announced that the Reverend Philip J. Wren had passed away in his sleep at the municipal albergue in Logroño on 1 May, 2013. A special mass was dedicated to Phil and offered for the repose of his soul at the noon Pilgrim Mass at the Cathedral in Santiago. In addition, his family was awarded his third Compostela for having completed the Camino a third time.

I later determined from a variety of sources, that Phil had succumbed to a massive heart attack in his sleep. His remains, as well as all of his gear including his camera equipment, was returned to his family in England.

This all made me very, very sad, at least until I put it all together. Phil KNEW that something was up. He was an ordained minister, and a profoundly religious person. I came to learn that he had a deep relationship with his God.

To this day, I still get chicken skin (aka goose bumps) when I recall Phil and I chatting in front of the municipal albergue at Logroño, and him telling me "…this is where (his) Camino ends. My journey is done." I cannot help but think that Phil knew he would not see his family on this side of the life to come.

I think Phil's faith was very strong. I still feel his presence, as well as his absence, to this day.

Update and Afterward

Some weeks later, the Camino Forum group members acted to collect funds to plant a memorial tree and place an engraved memorial plaque to remember Phil on the Camino Francés. Many forum members contributed and Rebekah Scott, one of the veteran forum members living on the Meseta in Moratinos, arranged to have a tree planted to provide shade to passing pilgrims just off the senda / trail on an otherwise treeless portion of the Meseta.

In May 2014, I had the distinct privilege and honor to visit Rebekah Scott at her Moratinos home. Together, we cemented and blessed the engraved plaque at the base of Phil's tree. It remains there flourishing to this day. This is discussed in a separate story about a memorial for Rev. Phil.

16

Do Vultures Really Eat Humans?
Pyrenees, France

May 2013 (P)

I first learned of this story AFTER I had walked beyond the previous story's place, in Logroño. While geographically out of place, I am recounting the story as I heard it. I had already walked about a week on the Camino Francés.

The Pyrenees are a range of mountains in southwest Europe forming a natural barrier and border between Spain and France. Reaching a maximum height of 3,404 meters (11,168 ft) altitude at the peak of Aneto, the range separates the Iberian Peninsula from the rest of continental Europe and extends for about 491 km (305 mi) from the Bay of Biscay (Cap Higuer) to the Mediterranean Sea (Cap de Creus).

For the most part, the main crest of this mountain range forms a divide between Spain and France with the tiny country of Andorra sandwiched in between. The Basque Country straddles the western Pyrenees. Historically, the Principality of Catalonia, the Kingdom of Aragón, Occitania, and the Kingdom of Navarre extended on both sides of the mountain range.

Several passes through the higher mountains permit travelers an easier passage from north to south from France into Spain. There are essentially four mountain passes. The eastern most passage is the foothills of the Pyrenees where the mountain chain reaches the Mediterranean Sea at Cape de Creus. The western passage is, similarly, where the western foothills of the mountain chain runs into the Atlantic Ocean at or near the Bay of Biscay at Cap Higuer.

There are passes through the Pyrenees mountains near the French towns of Somport and Saint Jean Pied de Port. These places are frequented by pilgrims on the Camino de Santiago making their way from the northern side of the Pyrenees coming from all over Europe to the destination of their pilgrimage at Santiago de Compostela in the Province of Galicia some 800 kilometers or more to the west.

As a practical matter, the Pyrenees also provide abundant opportunities for outdoor sports including skiing, climbing, and hiking. In particular, hiking is very popular with local residents and groups. Both Spanish and French residents enjoy spending time in the forested slopes and the incredible views from the mountain tops above the tree line.

On the mountain paths and passes, in the forests and on the pastures in this mountain range are many varieties of wild and domesticated farm animals. Cows, sheep, goats, and small horses known as Pottock horses are abundant. The pasture land is very lush and these animals can readily be seen up close. Farmers have been raising animals on these lands for many hundreds of years.

The next part of setting the stage for this story follows.

The griffon vulture is a large vulture and is a bird of prey. It is also known as the Eurasian griffon. Adult wingspans can exceed two meters, or about seven feet.

Like other vultures, it is a scavenger feeding mostly from carcasses of dead animals which it finds by soaring over open areas often moving in flocks. It establishes nesting colonies in mountain cliffs undisturbed by humans while soaring over open areas and scavenging dead animals within dozens of kilometers of their cliffside nests.

More recently, the Pyrenees griffon vulture population has been affected by a European Union (EU) ruling that, due to danger of Bovine Spongiform Encephalopathy (BSE) or Mad Cow Disease transmission, no dead animal carcasses are permitted to remain in high pasture of fields where the vultures traditionally scavenged them.

The EU ruling required that carcasses be collected and either incinerated or well buried. The griffon vulture was part of the symbiotic relationship in nature for hundreds or thousands of years. It derived the bulk of its regular diet by cleaning up dead animals left in fields for any reason.

Although the griffon vulture does not normally attack larger living prey, there are reports of Spanish griffon vultures killing weak, young or unhealthy living animals as they do not find enough carrion to eat. The EU ruling forced these birds of prey to start to go after domestic pets in residential areas and virtually anything edible that they could scavenge to survive.

This sets the stage for the rest of this story.

In early May 2013, I was making my way across northern Spain on the Camino de Santiago for the first time. I do not recall exactly where I was at the time, but at one daily refreshment stop I overheard other pilgrims talking about the woman that was eaten by vultures while on Camino. Okay, THIS got my attention. I had seen and admired many herds and flocks of wild animals on my passage across the Pyrenees. I also saw and admired the beautiful vultures as they soared through the high mountain areas. They had huge wingspans and were very majestic birds.

The very next time I had access to free Wi-Fi, I fired up my web browser and searched for "vulture Pyrenees dead woman." What I learned was both shocking and very interesting. The story was carried on 5 and 6 May in multiple news outlets all over the world. My recounting of this sad story is a composite of having read all those news accounts.

During the middle of April 2013, three French women set on a day hike in the Pyrenees. They were not on the Camino de Santiago. Rather, they were walking near the Pic de Pista well inside France near the town of Larrau. This is some 50 kilometers (about 30 miles) east of Saint Jean Pied de Port, and the route of the Camino Francés. But it was definitely in the neighborhood. As a large bird flies, so to speak, 30 miles or 50 kilometers is not far at all.

Anyway, while walking a narrow trail with a steep drop off, one of the day hikers, a 52-year old woman, evidently took a shortcut. On her way, she lost her footing and fell off the path. She fell approximately 300 meters or about 1,000 feet down a steep slope before coming to a stop. Local authorities believed she likely died in the fall.

Her walking companions immediately called the 112 standard emergency number to summon help. It took about 40 to 50 minutes for first responders to access the remote location from below where the woman had fallen.

As recounted in the various news accounts I read then, and just re-searched when I wanted to set this story down, the leader of the responder team commented that they used a helicopter to search for the fallen hiker. While doing so, they saw numerous vultures on the ground without realizing what they (the vultures) were doing.

By the time the first responders could get to the fallen woman the 52-year-old's woman's bones, clothes and shoes were all that remained after being set upon by the griffon vultures. The vultures had devoured the body in just 40 minutes. One can only pray that she did break her neck and die in the fall. The alternative is simply too horrid to consider.

I conclude that yes, a hungry griffon vulture will eat you if it thinks you are either dead or badly injured. They are indigenous in the Pyrenees mountain region and overlay with some Camino routes. These routes include the Camino del Norte, Camino Francés, and Camino Aragonés, among lesser routes.

More importantly, EU government rules for disposing of dead farm animals have caused the griffon vultures to become more desperate and less choosy about their next meal.

This is one of those things that I likely would not have believed unless I had knowledge of it, even be it third-hand. The story is very sad but true.

17

Need a Massive Pedicure
Burgos, Spain

May 2013 (P)

This story is also out of strict chronological sequence but I do not think it matters. While walking after Pamplona, I noticed that my right foot was starting to hurt. The heel hurt like it was on fire. Every step I took was become more tender and painful.

After a couple of days, I found myself only able to take small, tender steps. One night I examined my foot after showering and detected a very thick callus on the outside of my right foot. It hurt because a blood-filled pocket was forming under the callus.

This is something I should have foreseen and addressed before my Camino. Over multiple years, and several Caminos, including about 3,000 kilometers of walking, I have never had a single blister on either of my feet. In this regard, I am both very lucky and very obsessive about taking care of my feet and what I wear on them.

This serious callus issue is created by the fact that like most people my feet are not symmetrical. They are not identical. Moreover, one of my legs and foot are outside the normal range of matching the other. My left leg and foot is correctly aligned and this foot does not give me any specific problems.

I did not find out until this trip that my right foot is about 5 degrees off-center pointing out and the foot is rotated a few degrees off level. The end result is that the right outer heel of my right foot grows extremely thick and painful calluses. Also, I was seeing, after a week or so of daily walking, that a blood-filled pocket was developing under the thick callus.

The next pharmacy I came upon I went into to explain as best I could that I had thick callus (talón fuerte) and needed to reduce it. They sold me a foot file. This was sort of a big piece of sandpaper on a plastic stick. I started using it every night after showering to reduce the callus.

I was already using Vaseline each morning to lubricate my feet before booting up. This moisturized my feet, prevented conventional blisters, but did not really stop the calluses from continuing to grow.

Each day it hurt a little more. I would wash, sand, then sand some more. I started using Vaseline on my feet before sleeping, putting on a pair of clean liner socks that I would wear the next day under my thick, cushioned woolen socks.

By the time I got to Santo Domingo de la Calzada, I was shuffling more than walking. Each step was painful. A physiotherapist who was massaging pilgrims' feet told me that I needed either a very good pedicure to get rid of all the callus, or to find a foot doctor. When I asked him where I would be best able to do this, he said that Burgos, three more walking days, would be the best place.

Not speaking much Spanish at all, I made some command decisions. First, I used the internet to make a hotel reservation at a four-star business hotel in Burgos. From 30 plus years of global traveling, I knew this would guarantee fluent English-speaking desk staff. I knew these folks could arrange for the services I might need. The next thing I did was figure out the bus schedule for leaving Santo Domingo de la Calzada the next day, a Saturday.

After visiting the chickens in the church, a long story about a medieval miracle that is in all Camino guidebooks so I will not repeat it here, I had a nice dinner and got to sleep. The next morning, I leap-frogged by bus, some 73 km farther west to Burgos. I did return the following year to walk this segment I was forced to miss.

On arrival at Burgos, I hobbled from the bus station to my hotel up behind the Cathedral. As I walked in with my shuffling pace, I got the attention of the two people behind the counter. I asked "Habla ingles?" and was greeted with, "Yes, we speak English here." Whew! My experience was once again proved.

I explained to these folks that I had thick callus on one foot with blood underneath, and I was increasingly unable to walk. I explained that I took a bus here from Santo Domingo to find one of three things:

- The world's best pedicure,

- A podiatrist; or,

- A taxi to take me to a local hospital emergency room.

They assured me they were happy to help and would get right on it. They checked me into my room late on Saturday morning. I had decided to stay the weekend so I had made a two-night reservation.

I got to my room, got unpacked and put my sports sandals on putting my hiking boots into a shopping bag.

Not 15 minutes later, the desk called and said that Dr. Martinez would see me at 11:45, in 20 minutes. In only that much time they had found a podiatrist to see me at midday on a Saturday.

I walked the 10 minutes to the address I was given, and pushed the buzzer to be admitted. A gentleman answered the intercom and spoke only Spanish. I was able to give my name and state that the hotel called. He buzzed me in.

I quickly came to find out that Doctor Martinez was an older man (in his 70s) who came into town to open his office on a day off just to tend to me. WOW! His walls were filled with plaques from all his education and experience events. Included were documents indicating that as a younger man, he was the regimental podiatrist for the Spanish Army parachute regiment. Clearly, this fellow had the experience and knowledge I needed.

Doctor Martinez pantomimed for me to get on the table, remove my socks and roll over for his examination. He checked my hiking boots pulled out the expensive Superfeet insoles I had been wearing, exclaimed, "BASURA!" and tossed the expensive pair of insoles into the nearest trash bin. Okay! Let's see what comes next. This is already interesting.

The kind doctor was hemming and hawing, and mumbling to himself. He produced a graphic to explain the congenital (from birth) misalignment of my foot. He explained, as best I could understand, that this is what caused the foot to make very heavy callus tissue. The insoles I was wearing only made it worse by rubbing the outer edge of the foot.

He went on to pantomime that he could fix this. Fine. He bid me to roll over again while he rolled a treatment tray under my feet. The next sensation was a cold liquid. I looked down to see my right foot, now yellow with Betadine surgical sanitizer liquid. Now I knew this was going to get really interesting. I saw scalpels, gauze, tubes and syringes. Yikes!

The next thing I see is the kind doctor drawing a clear liquid into a disposable syringe. All I can think to ask is "Disculpeme señor doctor, que es esto? (Excuse me doctor, what it this?) He looks at me with one of those magnifier mirror things we used to see on 1960s TV doctor shows on his head, while holding the tiny bottle and syringe and says loudly, "LI-DO-CAHN-YA." Oops, Lidocaine. Now things are going to get really interesting.

For 20 minutes, the kind doctor is mumbling to himself about things being "muy mal" (very bad), "menos mal" (less bad) "no mal" (not bad) and finally "mucho major" (much better). It did not hurt, but he was happily carving and digging away. At one point, the relief was clear, and I figured that he must have drained the blood-filled pocket and relieved the pressure.

Finally, I feel gauze and tape being applied. The doctor bids me roll over and sit up. He explains, in Spanish of course, like I might understand what he did. I sort of followed what he was doing even though I was face down on the table for most of it. I grasped the mechanics of it. He had numbed my foot, carved the callus off, drained and irrigated the open wound, then dressed the wound with antibacterial ointment and securely dressed it.

The doctor told me (pantomime and simple Spanish – as I was a relative idiot) that I could not walk the Camino for three days, that I should return in two days, on Monday, to see him, and that he would have a new insole for me then. Then I asked him how much. When he said €70, I almost fainted. Back home, the services I just had would have cost several hundred dollars easily. I was thrilled to pay him.

I hobbled back to the hotel and did not do much walking around in my sports sandals. But and as mentioned in an earlier story, I did spend a couple of rest days at Burgos playing tourist. It was very enjoyable. Burgos is a very beautiful and very historic city.

On Monday, I returned to Doctor Martinez as instructed. He got me on the table and removed the dressings. From his mumbling and single words, he was clearly pleased with the results. Finally, all he said to me was, "Manaña, el Camino okay!" The last word was the ONLY English I got out of him.

He gave me a set of custom, cork and felt insoles he produced for me, by hand, it only fit the heel and arch but would last me the rest of the trip.

When I asked about the cost, he said €40. Again, I was floored. I would have been more than happy to pay any price for the relief he gave me. He literally saved my Camino. I shook his hand and even gave him a very appreciative "man hug." I was VERY impressed.

Among the things he explained to me on my first visit two days earlier was that, when he was a younger man, he too had walked the entire Camino Francés. Because of this he had a special respect and affinity for all pilgrims. That is why he came into his office on a day off to help me. I was speechless, something very rare for me. He brought tears to my eyes. Surely this was the Camino spirit.

This did highlight several things that I have come to understand and share with others. The Camino experience is special. Being a pilgrim creates a shared bond among persons from all walks of life, all nationalities, religions, etc. Pilgrims seem to just go out of their way to help another pilgrim in need. We all realize that we have been there and done that. We live the Golden Rule, we do unto others as we would have them do unto us.

The following morning, a Tuesday, I ended my three day stay at Burgos and headed out to the west. More adventures and experiences were to follow.

18

We Are Going to Need to Lance That

Vega de Valcarce, León, Spain

May 2013 (P)

Several days before arriving at the historic settlement of O'Cebreiro, I was walking with several new friends. One of these was a lady I will call Rita who was from Switzerland near Lucerne. Rita grew up hiking in the Alps and I was frequently hard-pressed to match her pace.

One of my other companions was a woman I will call Grace who was a nurse back in Australia. Grace had been helping me distribute my warm hats all along the Camino to this point. We made a friendly little team. Though they would typically stay in albergues and I in commercial lodging to avoid getting ill, we would meet again each following day to share the day's experiences.

One day, Rita told us she had a sore on her leg and she was concerned it might be infected. She recounted that she had been bitten by an insect two weeks earlier. When the sore did not get better, she went to a local Centro de Salud (Health Center – or community health clinic). There, a doctor examined her wound, gave her Paracetamol (acetaminophen) and told her to watch the wound if it did not get better. Well, of course, a generic pain reliever was not going to cure an infection.

Several days later with the wound now looking like an angry pustule, she went to a second Centro de Salud. They did

87

the exact same thing as the first place.

Both Grace and I examined the wound and we agreed that: (a) whatever it was, it was infected. There were now striations or subdued streaks extending down her leg from the wound. And, (b) we agreed that the proper course of action was to lance, and drain, dress the wound. An antibiotic ought to be provided as well.

I happened to have a reservation at one of my favorite places on that stretch of the Camino Francés. In Vega de Valcarce there is a chain truck-stop. There one can obtain a spotless hotel -style room with a private bath for less than Euro 30 per night. The rooms are huge, have bathtubs, and typically two beds.

We arrived there, I checked into my reserved room and the two ladies got a room together. It turned out that each room had a patio with a stainless-steel café style patio table set. This was to be the perfect operating theatre.

After getting unpacked, washing and doing the laundry, we met with all of our medical kit on the ladies' room patio. I had alcohol wipes which I used to sanitize the table top. Among the three of us, we had gauze pads, medical tape, antibiotic ointment, and I even had a full course of two different antibiotics.

I had started with three separate antibiotics but had consumed the Z-Pack (azithromycin) to treat my bronchitis at Pamplona. I had a full course of Amoxicillin and Ciprofloxacin (Cipro).

As we were getting set up, I asked Rita if she was allergic to any antibiotic. She said no, so I asked Grace - the nurse - which of the two available full courses of antibiotic would be most appropriate for an infected leg wound. The Cipro was chosen. Fine by me.

The next consideration was what to use as a scalpel. I had a very sharp Swiss Army knife and a cigarette lighter to sterilize it with. However, for liability reasons, I had some second thoughts about using my knife. I did not mind donating the prescription antibiotic.

These prescriptions were provided by my US doctor as a just-in-case thing. As they were not a controlled substance, like a narcotic, any law I was breaking was a tiny infraction not likely a big deal. Besides, Rita was looking at a serious infection and possible blood poisoning if we did not act.

In the end, Rita produced her own wicked sharp Swiss Army knife. I contributed the lighter to sterilize the blade, and agreed that Grace, the nurse, would be the surgeon. If this sounds involved, it was. Lancing a swollen pustule, the size of a green pea is not to be taken lightly. The first doctor she saw should have drained, irrigated, cleaned and dressed the wound, and should have given her an antibiotic instead of Paracetamol.

Cutting to the chase, Grace sliced the pustule open, I swabbed with sterile gauze pads. Yuk! Grace used alcohol wipes to sterilize and clean out the open wound. We applied an antibiotic ointment, then Grace dressed the wound with gauze and tape.

Finally, I gave Rita the antibiotic tablets and told her she needed to take one now, one before going to sleep, and two each day, every day, starting tomorrow, until the entire 10-day supply was gone. Even though her spoken English was excellent, I wanted to make certain she understood the prescription instructions.

The next morning, we walked up to O' Cebreiro. However, along the way, Rita happened upon a stout, handsome fellow from Hungary who she had befriended earlier in her Camino. Evidently love was in the air. Neither Grace nor I saw Rita again for some time as she loped off together with her gentleman friend.

What happens on the Camino, stays on the Camino…

Interesting Names and The Last Hat
Before Triacastela, Galicia, Spain

May 2013 (P)

Walking from O'Cebreiro to Triacastela, I found myself encountering very cold weather with snow most mornings especially at higher altitudes. Most any mountain at least 700 meters above sea level could see some snow through late May. In fact, at the café just before the Alto do Poio, I gave away my last microfleece cap.

At this café stop, many pilgrims gathered for a morning coffee after walking from O'Cebreiro. While adjusting my gear, I saw a young couple who were in some distress. The young woman was fine, but her male walking companion was clearly ill. He was underdressed for the weather and seemed to have a really bad cold or something similar.

I turned to my walking companion and asked her to pull the last microfleece cap from the mesh panel on my rucksack. I passed it to the woman who spoke some English to give to her friend who spoke none. When she realized what the item was and how much her friend needed it, she started to cry. She said they had no money to repay me. I explained this was a gift. More tears. I told her to just do something kind for another pilgrim in need.

Then I gave the fellow a full roll of Hall's Mentholyptus cough drops. He clearly needed them to alleviate his congestion symptoms. Neither of these pilgrims had ever seen these before. I explained that they were similar to the popular European Ricola aromatic cough drops but much stronger. Again, more tears. We started as strangers and parted as friends.

Walking towards Triacastela, I encountered a group of young men who appeared to be in a group but all strung out along the trail. As is typically the situation, when a pilgrim walks up to another pilgrim the standard "good morning," "good afternoon," etc., is stated in English or then Spanish. If one is not starting a conversation, one usually says, "Buen Camino" and walks on.

In this case I found this young man to be interesting. I introduced myself. He said his name was Richard and that he was from Germany. I found that interesting as I had never met a Richard from Germany. I politely asked if Richard was an alternative for Reichart or perhaps Reinhart. He said no. His parents wanted him to have a strong Anglo-Saxon name as he hoped to have an international career. Having an English-friendly name would be an asset. I allowed that made a lot of sense.

When I lived in Belgium, friends of mine had a son they named Dean, after the American movie star James Dean. The reasoning was pretty much the same. In each case, the parents wanted the child to have every advantage, and to not be in any way encumbered by an identifiably ethnic name. They wanted him to have a strong unambiguous name.

I asked if he was with a group. Richard stated that he was walking with his father. We chatted a bit more, then I wished him a Buen Camino and walked on towards Triacastela.

Following my brief conversation with Richard, I continued towards Triacastela. The views as you come down the hills into the valley are wonderful. At that point in Galicia, the countryside looks just like Ireland. It is very green. The fields are small and all bordered by stone walls. There are cows and sheep grazing on the hillsides. It is truly a picture book view.

As I am walking along, I encounter a man walking solo and dressed in black. I greeted him and we start a chat. When we introduced ourselves, and he said his name was Hanjo (han-joe). Now, that was a most unusual name.

He indicated he was from a very small village in Germany, and that was the name his parents had given him. He said that names like that were not uncommon in some rural areas.

We chatted at more length and I asked him what he did back in Germany. Hanjo said he had been a CMC operator. My father was a machinist most of his career. Although he was a hands-on, old school, machinist, I knew what a computerized milling console machine was. Hanjo operated one of these.

It made for a very interesting conversation. As he explained how everything worked, I understood everything. I was even able to ask intelligent questions because of the many things my father had taught me about being a machinist. Many of the terms and processes were still in use, albeit now controlled precisely by computers.

We had a very pleasant conversation. We finally arrived at Triacastela and I headed for my lodgings and Hanjo towards his. We bid one another Buen Camino.

This story about Richard and Hanjo is a piece of the puzzle that finally comes together in a week or so. Just remember this part of the story.

20

Heidi, Watch Out for The Bull!

After Sarria, Galicia, Spain

May 2013 (P)

After leaving Sarria on the final segment of the Camino Francés towards Santiago de Compostela, one walks through tiny villages or hamlets. Many of these small places have more farm animals than people.

I cannot recall how it occurred or exactly where we were, but I was reunited with Rita, the lady from Switzerland, and Grace, the nurse from Australia. Rita's gentleman friend from Hungary was nowhere to be seen. We were walking along a country path with pastures to each side. The pastures were separated by stone walls and had a strand or two of barbed wire to keep the animals in.

As we are walking, with me slightly ahead, I hear cow bells. Rita goes all kiddie-excited on us and proceeds to drop her rucksack, and hop over the wall and wire into the pasture. She is giddy with joy shouting to us that growing up in Switzerland she used to play with the cows in the pastures and they all wore bells just like these cows. Grace and I referred to this as Rita going all "Heidi" on us, Heidi being the star of a famous classic story about people living in the Swiss Alps.

There were perhaps a dozen cows in the walled and fenced off pasture. Rita was greeting each of them as though they were long lost friends. Grace and I were watching this, not quite believing our eyes.

Then, I saw an odd commotion in the left rear corner of the pasture. We had all missed the one bull that was in the pasture with all the other dozen or so cows. As I was watching this bull, he started to behave aggressively. Clearly, he has seen Rita frolicking with HIS cows. It appeared that the bull found this unacceptable. I was watching Rita playing with the cows with one eye while watching the bull with the other.

The bull was scuffing his front paws while lowering his head with his horns, and making huffing noises.

I told Grace we needed to get Rita out of there before the bull did something Rita would definitely regret.

We both called out to Rita that there was a bull in the pasture and he was not happy. No one was more surprised than Rita. She had missed it, too. We told her to calmly, but quickly, make her way back to the stone wall and hop back over.

Of course, nothing is ever easy. It was easier for Rita to get over the wall into the pasture, than it was to get out. As she was strolling slowly, the bull started trotting. Now we told her to hurry as the bull was coming her way.

At this point, Rita saw the bull, uttered something, likely profane in her native German, and started to run for the wall. The trotting bull became a galloping bull. Grace and I dropped our rucksacks and climbed part way over the wall.

As Rita approached the wall, we each grabbed an arm and pulled her up and over the wall. Not a second after she was back on the safe side, the bull got to the stone wall and came to an abrupt stop. He was still agitated, huffing and puffing, and scuffing his front paws on the grass.

We pulled Rita to her feet and I shook my finger in her face and said, "Young lady. Do not ever do anything like that again…ever! This Heidi routine has to stop." By the way, Rita was in her early 70s. This made her actions both all the more understandable and far more amusing.

Pssst, You Wanna Volunteer – Maybe?

Santiago de Compostela, Galicia, Spain

May 2013 (P)

After some 37 days, I finally arrived at Santiago de Compostela for the first time. Over my entire Camino, I had daily rain or snow on 24 of 37 days. Today was no different. Drizzle and cold. I was wearing my hiking raincoat with hood all buttoned and zipped-up to stay as warm and dry as possible.

The old center of Santiago de Compostela is magical. The Cathedral is about 800 years old, so many of the surrounding buildings are nearly as old. When you come from a country that is only about 250 years old, this is amazing. I am sure I looked like the lost country boy in the city for the first time. To me, everything I saw was new and different. Walking on the ancient paving stones was a unique experience for me.

I followed the signs and the map I had and finally came to Rúa do Vilar 3. At that time, this was the location of the Pilgrim Office. It was located in an old pazo or fancy city house. Owned by the Cathedral, it was put to use to receive pilgrims. I entered through the gates off the street into the courtyard. Directly ahead were the former stables to hold horses and carriages for the former residents. Now, the ground floor had bathrooms for men and women.

The entry to the Pilgrim Office proper was through a door to the right where one had to queue on a stairway. The office was at the top of this stairs. I got in the line and waited as the queue advanced for each pilgrim processed.

As I got near the top there was this burly American chatting up the arriving pilgrims. He was wearing a blue t-shirt with the word "Welcome" printed in white in perhaps seven languages. On the back it read "Amigo." Okay, I got that much. I am a friend and I welcome you. So far so good. Plus, this fellow did speak English.

We introduced ourselves. He asked where I had walked from. I told him. He asked if I had ever considered volunteering. "Huh, what?" was my initial reply, as his question came out of the blue, or grey sky, as I was standing out in the light rain.

I thought briefly then replied: "Let's see, I have just walked about 500 miles over the Pyrenees to this place for the first time. It has rained or snowed for 24 of the past 37 days. I am cold, wet, exhausted and I seriously need a cold beer, so I have not considered volunteering. But thank you for asking."

He then went on to tell me how it is a great job. The housing is free, the people are wonderful and the experience is well worth it. He also said that he got far more out of the experience than the effort he put into it. Okay, okay, I give up. "How would I go about volunteering, if I were interested?"

He told me. First, I had to be a member of the American Pilgrims on the Camino (APOC). Check, already did that. Second, I had to have completed any full Camino. Check, just did that. Third, each year, in the fall, APOC puts out a call for volunteers. They receive and do a front-end assessment to see that volunteers meet the basic requirements. Then they forward their list onto the Amigo program coordinator here in Santiago. I can do that, after returning home.

With that information, I was finally able to get to the top of the stairs and present myself for my first Compostela. That went very easily, and I was pleased with myself when I left with my "credencial" stamped and my Compostela in hand.

Now, off I go to find my lodgings. That year I had reservations at a nice hotel in the Bonaval section of the city just outside the entry to the old town and up the hill slightly to the left. Although I learned to loathe walking backwards to cover the same terrain twice, this was worth it as I was DONE.

22

Your Voice Sounds Familiar, HUH!

Santiago de Compostela, Galicia, Spain

May 2013 (P)

Having arrived in Santiago de Compostela and obtained my Compostela the previous day, I set about performing the rest of the pilgrim welcome ritual.

Traditionally, this includes climbing the stairs to the right side-rear of the great altar to perform the abrazo or hug of the Apostle Saint. This is where you climb the stairs and take a moment to hug a larger-than-life-size statue of Santiago, and his jewel encrusted cape, to utter a prayer of thanks for supporting you in your journey to this point.

The second part of this ritual is to proceed from the abrazo of the Apostle Saint to the crypt beneath the great altar. Approximately under the great altar, are the remains of the original walls of the first-century Roman necropolis / crypt where the remains of the great saint and his two followers, Thaddeus and Athanasius, were discovered around AD 844 by the hermit monk Pelayo.

There is a large, solid silver casket or rectangular box containing three smaller but ornate wooden boxes. The silver casket is perhaps a meter long by half a meter high and wide. Any way you look at it, it is BIG. Each of the wooden boxes contain the bones of a complete skeleton except that the box containing the Apostle Saint's remains / relics lacks a skull.

The record does reflect that James the Apostle was beheaded by sword in the year AD 44. The other two boxes contain the skeletal remains of Thaddeus and Athanasius, his two followers.

There used to be a third part of the standard pilgrim ritual. That involved placing one's hand in the indented, hand shape worn through millions of such actions in the Pillar of Jesse located at the Pórtico de la Gloria on the western façade and main entry to the cathedral. If you saw the film *The Way*, this scene was permitted, but only for the movie. Regrettably, this is no longer permitted.

Beyond obtaining my Compostela, saying thank you to the Apostle Saint and venerating his relics in the crypt, I had other things to do at the Cathedral…

The Plenary Indulgence (also known as "The Jubilee") – I copied this information directly from the Pilgrim Office website at: https://oficinadelperegrino.com/en/pilgrimage/plenary-indulgence/

"The doctrine and practice of indulgences in the Catholic Church are closely linked to the Sacrament of Reconciliation (confession). An indulgence is the full remission of all temporal punishment (time spent in purgatory) up to that point in a person's life. Individuals can gain Plenary Indulgences for themselves and also for the deceased.

"To gain the Jubilee Indulgence individuals must:

- Visit the Cathedral of Santiago where lies the Tomb of St. James the Great.

- Say a prayer: at least the Apostle's Creed, the Our Father and a prayer for the intentions of the Pope.

- It is also recommended that the individual attend Mass.

- Receive the Sacrament of Reconciliation (go to

confession) and Eucharist (go to communion) within the 15-days before or after the visit to the Cathedral.

Indulgences can be gained at other times in the year through the performance of other acts of devotion. These are outlined in the Catechism of the Catholic Church."

While there remains an active debate within the Camino community as to whether this indulgence can only be obtained during a designated Holy Year, I was not going to pass up the opportunity, just in case. A Holy Year occurs in any year where the Feast of Santiago, on 25 July, falls on a Sunday. This occurred in 2010 and will again in 2021.

In plain language, this means that the time you would have to spend in Purgatory atoning even for forgiven sins is wiped away. Your soul becomes as pure as the day you were baptized or christened into the Church.

If you did all the things itemized above, then got taken out by a meteor on your way out of the Cathedral, Catholic Church dogma says you go directly to Heaven... with no time remaining to be served in Purgatory. Clearly, for your run of the mill Cradle Catholic forgiven but repeat sinner like me this is a BIG deal.

Being an organized sort of fellow, I hugged the statute and thanked Santiago, proceeded to venerate his relics in the crypt, then set out to find a priest to hear my confession, in English. One of the wonderful things about Santiago de Compostela is that it is home to the University of Santiago de Compostela (USC). This is a very old Catholic university and there are many priests on the academic staff. These priests are predominantly from Spain, but there are many priests from countries around the world. These priests are seconded to hear confessions, say the Mass, or provide other pastoral services to the global community of pilgrims all arriving at Santiago.

In the Cathedral, there were at the time fourteen old-fashioned very ornate wooden confessional boxes. They are freestanding on the ancient stones. A priest sits in the middle, with kneeling positions on either side for penitents. Priests post a sign indicating the languages they can hear confessions in. It is amazing to see the scope of languages available to penitents on any given day.

Typically, Spanish, Portuguese, Italian and French are available most all the time. But English is frequently available. I have seen signs for priests offering to hear confession in Polish, Ukrainian, Lithuanian, Chinese, Korean and Japanese. Some of these are only available when a visiting professor priest is available. It is clear that the Cathedral is trying to accommodate everyone possible.

Wandering around in the mid-morning, I found a confessional with a priest who offered confession in German, French and English. Close enough for me. I got in the short queue a few meters away from one side of the box.

After maybe fifteen minutes, my turn came. I kneeled and prepared to go through the ritual as I had done hundreds of time over my life. The door slid open on the inside of the confessional (the priest's side). He greeted me in German, I asked, "English bitte?" (German for English please) … and we were off. I am doing my part of the ritual and the priest is doing his part.

About 20 or 30 seconds into things, all of a sudden, the priest interrupts me and says "Excuse me, but your voice sounds familiar." WHAT? Talk about a very weird moment. He follows with "Did you just come off Camino?" Now I am faced with the choice of being cute, after all I am thinking, like - what would I be doing here otherwise? OR, just answering the question respectfully. Discretion wins out. I reply, "Yes, Father." But I am starting to feel a little bit uneasy with the direction this is taking. After all, I have done this ritual many, many times over the decades, and no priest ever went off script like this.

What comes next makes my hair stand up. The priest asks "Were you by any chance the fellow who was handing out warm hats to pilgrims who needed them?" BIG GULP! What the heck is going on here? Now I am waiting for a lightning bolt to come and take me out. Again, a lifetime of Catholic conditioning compels me to simply answer, "Yes, Father." But inside I am very anxious, glancing for either a camera or that lightning bolt.

He goes on to tell me that, "Your good deeds were seen and noticed." NOW I am really waiting for that lightning bolt. He asked what made me do this. All I could say was that I lacked a warm hat early on, and found one to satisfy my need. When I did, I got the sudden thought that others might have been similarly caught unawares of the late winter that year and be in need. The decision to buy a bunch of hats just seemed like the right thing to do.

He asked how many I had handed out. My answer was that I started with a dozen at Pamplona, had given several to my pilgrim family early on, replenished my supply with another eight or ten at Ponferrada, and gave the last one out at Alto do Poio. He replied that was the one he personally witnessed, when I gave the hat and Halls Mentholyptus cough lozenges to the young man who clearly needed them. I did not see any priests lurking about, just other pilgrims. It just goes to prove that your never know who is watching you.

At that point, the priest says we should finish the confession ritual and would I come around to his side of the box afterwards as he wanted to give me his card. Fine by me. I am still looking to each side for the lightning bolt. This is several levels beyond weird.

We finished the rest of the ritual. The priest said I had already done my penance by making it here and in the good deeds I had done when no one was watching. He would impose no additional penance. Okay, fine by me. We concluded the ritual.

I stand up and walk around to the open-side and I see this fellow in wire rimmed glasses but now clean-shaven sitting there in a cassock and stole. I exclaim, "YOU! The CMC operator fellow with the odd name from Germany." He says, "Guilty as charged," then explains that he was escorting a group of young men, like young Richard who was walking with his "Father" if you recall several stories back. In my view, Richard could do well as a politician. Imagine, telling the truth without seeming to. Go figure!

His business card read Dr. Christopher 'Hanjo' Kollman and he is a professor on the USC staff. Fr. Kollman goes on to explain that he was born into the Lutheran tradition, and that is how he was given the local name that he earlier introduced himself to me with near Triacastela. He did work as a CMC mill operator before attending seminary. Everything he said to me on the Camino was technically truthful. When he later converted to Catholicism, he took the first name Christopher. He later received a vocation, attended seminary, and was ordained a Catholic priest.

I told him he had me going there. I explained that almost being 60 years old, I had done the confession ritual hundreds of times, and no priest ever went off script, at least nowhere near as far off script. We had a good laugh over that. I explained that, as he was asking questions, I was waiting for the lightning bolt to strike me dead. That made him laugh all the harder. We remaining in contact via e-mail for some months, then this slid away.

But I did remain for the noon Pilgrim Mass, including the Botafumeiro, received Communion, said the prayers for the Pope's intentions. Having ticked all those to-do-boxes off to be eligible for the Jubilee Indulgence, I am not sure what I was expecting. But I can tell you that bells did not ring for me, there was no thunder clap, doves, or beam of sunlight from Heaven. One moment I was spiritually flawed, and the next I was simply purified and saved – again.

23

Happy 60th Birthday to Me
Santiago de Compostela, Galicia, Spain

June 2013 (P)

If I recall correctly, I arrived at Santiago de Compostela on 3 June. My 60th birthday occurred two days later, on 5 June. I have already accounted for my first two days. It occurred to me that a good way to celebrate the first half of my life would be to attend the noon Pilgrim Mass on my birthday. In this thought, I was being optimistic, as I am a glass half-full sort of person. The plan was to arrive early to get a seat for the noon Pilgrim Mass.

I entered the Cathedral and was able to find a place to sit in the North Transept on the opposite side of the South Transept entry during the near-decade long Cathedral renovation. The noon Pilgrim Mass was celebrated, as it frequently is, with the swinging of the Botafumeiro after the Mass. How cool is that I thought. They got the Botafumeiro into action to help celebrate my birthday! Well, it seemed that way to me.

As the Mass ended and people stared making for the exits, across the Transept I spotted a familiar face. It was Michelle, the woman I had started out with at Saint Jean Pied de Port some 40 days earlier. This was the woman whose hiking pole I fixed on the first day and who kindly repaired my broken sleeping bag zipper on the second day.

After the first week or so on Camino, her very fast walking pace caused her to get way out in front of me and I never saw her again until that moment opposite me in the Cathedral. I hurried through the now empty pews to get nearer to her so I could call her without shouting in the Cathedral. Michelle was as surprised as I was to meet once again.

At that moment, I got an idea and told her that this was definitely serendipity or karma at work. There was a reason she was there at that point in time. I invited her to have lunch with me telling her that she was my birthday present. I never expected to see her again and this was a very welcome surprise.

We exited the Cathedral via the South Transept and turned to the left to find a café on the Plaza de Quintana. There are several very nice outdoor cafes there and if you catch it just right, you can hear the Jazzman of Santiago play jazz guitar. He has a plug-in amplifier and plays jazz music. We got lucky. We found a table in the sun and enjoyed our pizza and beer while the Jazzman played.

We spent an hour or so catching up on each other's Camino and post-Camino plans. Also, we exchanged e-mail addresses so we could remain in touch. We still do, to this day.

After our very pleasant lunch, Michelle and I decided to walk around to the front of the Cathedral to see who had ended up in the Plaza Obradoiro that day. I quickly learned that sooner or later, all pilgrims wind up here. In the center of the plaza is a bronze marker indicating that this is the zero-distance marker for measuring distance on all Camino routes ending at Santiago de Compostela.

This is where pilgrims end up on arriving at the Cathedral, and before or after they go to the Pilgrim Office. This is where all the selfie photographs and group photos are taken. Festivals and official events are celebrated here. It is the crossroads of the Camino.

So far, it was turning out to be a most pleasant 60th birthday.

However, I was to have one of the most profound experiences of my entire Camino experience as we walked from our café through Plaza Praterias towards the west façade of the Cathedral. It needs to be a separate story. Please bear with me.

24

"Dominick," Part I
Santiago de Compostela, Galicia, Spain

June 2013 (P)

Continuing to walk from the Plaza Praterías towards Plaza Obradoiro, Michelle and I are chatting and enjoying the sunny day, when all of a sudden, she screams out, "Dominick!" She tugs at my arm, and tells me I have to meet this fellow pilgrim.

Opposite us, walking the other way is a tall man, dressed in black from head to foot. He is carrying a single, long walking staff, and he apparently cannot walk normally. Michelle brings me over to introduce me to him.

We step to the side of the narrow street so others can pass and to stand in the precious shade. Michelle is going on about how brave and determined is Dominick. He is French from Alsace-Lorraine. He speaks far better English than I do French, so he explained his situation to me.

In 2010, three years earlier, he had a left-side stroke in his head. This caused profound paralysis in his right side. Dominick endured three years of intense physical rehabilitation. He determined that if God would help him improve his ability to walk, he vowed to make pilgrimage to Santiago to both give thanks and to seek the miracle of a more complete cure.

I mentioned Dominick was from the Alsace-Lorraine region of France. This region is in the northeast of France. Dominick had started his Camino from the steps of the Cathedral in Strasbourg, France, the major city of this province. He walked from Strasbourg to a cousin's home near Saint Jean Pied de Port.

After resting at his cousin's home for a couple of weeks, the cousin dropped him off at Saint Jean Pied de Port where he joined the other pilgrims headed west to Santiago de Compostela. But to understand the scope of this effort you need to know some other things about Dominick.

His three years of physical therapy got him to a point where he could walk by taking a normal step with his left foot, unaffected by the stroke, then place the long hiking staff a meter or more out in front. Dominick then partially lifted and dragged his right leg and foot to the staff. He used that dragging-leg gait to hike about 1,800 kilometers or nearly 1,100 miles, from Strasbourg to Santiago de Compostela.

Each morning, someone in the albergue he was staying at had to help Dominick get dressed. This was because his stroke had left his right hand permanently in a claw-like grip. He could not handle buttons, snaps or even Velcro closures very easily. While he could bathe and feed himself and tend to grooming chores, dressing posed unique difficulties. Once Dominick was dressed for the day, he stayed that way until he was ready to go to sleep. Then the dressing process was reversed, with the assistance of another pilgrim.

I was astonished! Along my Camino I had met people from many countries with many back-stories. There were quite a few people who were walking to give thanks after recovering from cancer, a heart attack, stroke, or some other malady. There were also many pilgrims who were religious and seeking a miracle cure for themselves or on behalf of another person.

But I never ever met anyone on any Camino or at Santiago de Compostela, then or since, who had the sheer audacity and perseverance that Dominick exhibited. I started to tear up as this all sank into me.

In my life, I had complained of pain, inconvenience or limitations due to injuries or disease. However, I had nothing, no problem whatsoever, that could ever possibly compare to the challenges that Dominick had to overcome to be there at Santiago de Compostela at that moment in time.

Michelle was thrilled to see Dominick again because, and as I mentioned earlier, she walked very fast. Clearly, Dominick could not. They got separated.

I asked Dominick why he walked. He previously had explained he was looking for the miracle of a more permanent cure. As we discussed this, he paused and thought about it some more. Then he stated that, where he had started this with the intention of giving thanks as well as to seek a miracle, he now realized that the miracle was that he actually made it some 1,800 kilometers on foot with minimal assistance.

Again, I was floored, astounded and emotionally affected as he said this. Dominick had the faith of one who could move mountains. I was at that moment, and remain to this day, in absolute awe of his accomplishment.

25

Becoming an Amigo
Northern Virginia, USA

January 2014 (V)

I had previously recounted how a volunteer Amigo working at the Pilgrim Office on my first arrival in 2013 put the notion of volunteering at the Pilgrim Office into my head. During the autumn of 2013, I watched the website of the American Pilgrims on Camino looking for an announcement about being a volunteer for the next year.

Eventually, late in the year, they posted a call seeking applications from interested persons. The information requested was fairly basic. It included identification information, an accounting of your Camino experiences and a description of your language skills. Knowledge of Spanish was emphasized.

I completed the information requested and sent my application. During January, I recall receiving an e-mail from a fellow named Johnnie Walker at Santiago telling me that I had been accepted as a volunteer for the 2014 season. He asked that I provide dates that I would be available.

At that point, I had been looking at planning another Camino but had not made any firm plans. This development changed that, and fast.

I decided I wanted to re-walk the Camino Francés with the specific purpose of walking those sections I had to use transportation to skip over to find medical care for my feet. I knew what route. Having been there and done that, I also knew when to start out from Saint Jean Pied de Port.

This, combined with my knowledge and experience from the previous year, caused me to propose arriving from Camino on or about Friday 29 May and being available for my volunteer assignment the following Monday, 1 June.

My proposed volunteer service dates were accepted and several housekeeping e-mail messages passed back and forth over the next few months. But I now had a plan and a purpose. To go with it, I had to plan my entire 2014 Camino working backwards from the dates we had agreed on.

And that is exactly what I did. Having learned so much the first year, planning the second pilgrimage was much easier.

26

A Memorial for Rev. Phil
Moratinos, Palencia, Spain

May 2014 (P)

Previously, I discussed how I met, walked with and befriended the Rev. Philip J. Wren during my first Camino in 2013. I also discussed how he passed away abruptly, and the general feeling of shock among the members of the English language Camino Forum in which he was a very frequent contributor under the user-name "MethodistPilgrim98."

In May of 2013, when news of his sudden and unexpected death hit all his friends and colleagues in the Camino Forum, it did not take long for someone to propose that we do something to memorialize his contributions and the admiration he was held in by the others in the Forum. After some back and forth discussion, Rebekah Scott, of Moratinos, offered to coordinate receiving contributions towards a tree and an engraved marker. Money was sent and plans were made.

In the autumn of 2013, Rebekah arranged to have a tree planted on a private farmer's field just before the hamlet of Moratinos near the end of the Meseta. The idea was, and remains, that Phil's memorial tree would grow large enough to provide much-needed shade to passing pilgrims in future. The tree is just at the edge of the farmer's field, about four meters off the senda / trail.

A search was made for a stonecutter who could produce the

desired engraved marker. While Spain has some of the world's finest craftsmen at this sort of thing, no local vendor could be found. Ultimately, Rebekah arranged with a stonecutter in the United Kingdom to engrave the stone.

The memorial stone was cut and engraved in early 2014. Another Forum member driving from the UK transported it to the Peaceable Kingdom (Rebekah's home) at Moratinos.

I learned this while I was planning my return to the Camino Francés for April and May 2014. Somewhere along the way, during the Forum dialogs and private e-mail I was asked if I might not be passing through Moratinos and would I be willing to help Rebekah cement the memorial stone in place at the base of the tree.

Of course, I immediately agreed and built an extra day into my plans for that stretch of the Camino. I arrived at Moratinos on 9 May, 2014, and stayed with Rebekah, her wonderful husband Paddy, and her menagerie of animals of many types.

The next day, 10 May 2014, Rebekah and I cemented the memorial stone in place at the base of Phil's tree. Rebekah very kindly held a brief ceremony for her and I to bless the stone. I had to imagine that Phil was smiling from above. It is a very fitting tribute.

I Meet Santa Claus, Really!
Santiago de Compostela, Galicia, Spain

June 2014 (V)

As planned, I ended my 2014 Camino at Santiago de Compostela on a Friday, and went to the Pilgrim Office the following Monday morning to begin a two-week volunteer stint. When I arrived, I met others with whom I would be working.

We were taken to an upstairs room to have a meeting about what was expected of us, the rules to be followed and what we would be doing. Included in our group of volunteers was a varied assortment of people this time all from the United States.

There was Ari from Miami who spoke fluent Portuguese and Spanish, in addition to English. He would be asked to work behind the counter interviewing arriving pilgrims.

Then there were Jack and Jill (my names for them). He was a professor from a U.S. college and had walked a Camino. Jill had not. She was what we called a tag along spouse. As Jack spoke fair Spanish, he was asked to work interviewing pilgrims, while Jill was asked to sell cardboard tubes / tubos to pilgrims to protect their Compostelas. These tubes have plastic caps on each end, in which one can roll-up one or more Compostelas to protect them in transit.

I was seriously deficient in Spanish language capability at that point in time. While I could survive on the Camino, my skills were in no way good enough to carry on a conversation with a native language speaker. I was asked to sell tubos, manage the queue, and generally, whatever else needed doing to help service the arriving pilgrims. That worked for me.

Then, there were Brad and Chere from Virginia, in the U.S. They were a fascinating couple. Brad had retired some years before from the U.S. Army, where he was a medical doctor with the rank of colonel. Brad had served more than 20 years in postings all over the world. A fascinating thing about Brad is that he was half Cherokee, the Native American tribe. As a very young child, his first babysitter happened to be a full Cherokee woman. The first language Brad learned as an infant was the Cherokee language from his babysitter. Then he learned English.

It got far more interesting. Evidently when the region of the developing brain that controls learning a language is stimulated by learning multiple languages at an early age, it sometimes has the ability to rapidly process, learn and integrate most any new language quickly later in life. This is what happened in Brad's case.

After he entered the U.S. Army as a young doctor, whatever country he would be assigned to, over the rest of his long career, he usually picked up the local language in four to six months. By the end of a year, he could speak it like a native. This is a gift that he developed to its fullest potential.

By the time I met Brad in June 2014 he could speak fluently, in addition to English and the Cherokee language: Spanish, French, German, Italian, and Turkish. He could also manage in Russian, Dutch and Portuguese fairly well. If I recall correctly, that is seven languages with fluency and another three with some conversational capability. This was to form the basis for some very funny days at the Pilgrim Office.

The other unique thing about Brad is that he looked EXACTLY like the American Thomas Nast commercialized version of Santa Claus. This is the Santa Claus that appears on Coca Cola products around the Christmas holidays, and is the version of the Saint Nicholas character we commonly use in the U.S.

On his retirement from the Army, Brad liked to tell people that his last promotion was from Colonel Brad to Santa Brad. He is SO right. After a few years, the beard and eyebrows grew to monumental length, and turned almost pure white. He retained enough of his hair on top to complete the look.

By the time he put on a few pounds, well maybe more than a few, all on his belly, he looked like a Santa Claus character from Hollywood central casting. Call for a Santa Claus, and you would get someone exactly like Brad.

Brad and his loving wife, Chere, leveraged the look to create Brad's retirement passion. He set out to offer his services to play Santa Claus anywhere, in any variant, and in almost any language. Over the years, he accumulated a complete set of costumes he could use to play ANY iteration of the historic Saint Nicholas character.

Some years later, I visited Brad and Chere at their home. They showed me his "Santa Cave…" He had one bedroom with a double closet, in which was one of every conceivable Saint Nicholas costume. These included:

- The original historic Saint Nicholas from the Turkey / Syria area

- Saint / Sint Nicholas, as celebrated in much of Western Europe

- Father Christmas from the United Kingdom

- Pere or Papa Noel, in France, Spain and Portugal

- Babbo Natale, as known in Italy

- Father Frost or Father Winter from Russia during the Soviet Union

The other thing to note was that Brad looked so much like the Thomas Nast caricature of Santa Claus that when we walked down the street in Williamsburg, Virginia, small children would stop, stare, get their parent's attention and point. Brad clearly had the look nailed…

Brad was hired to provide the standard holiday season character at embassy parties in the U.S. as he lived fairly near to Washington, D.C. If the Italian Embassy was having a party and wanted him, out came the Babbo Natale costume, and the Italian language. For a time, he was also the official Father Christmas at the U.S. colonial era reproduction village at Colonial Williamsburg, Virginia. Also, a major theme park chain in the U.S. made him the official Santa Claus at one of their major theme parks near Williamsburg.

That is great as it is. But remember, Brad could speak most all of these languages fluently. No matter what language a child might blurt out when sitting on Santa's lap, Brad could usually speak to them in their own language.

Chere usually helped by playing Mrs. Claus for those variants of the great Saint where a Mrs. Claus was appropriate. She even had her range of suitable costumes. What a pair! If there was ever a couple who espoused the Camino creed of generosity towards other pilgrims, who could possibly do a better job than Santa and Mrs. Claus?

Back to Santiago, where I did not know all of this on the first day. Things were about to get interesting and highly amusing.

28

Amigos!
Santiago de Compostela, Galicia, Spain

June 2014 (V)

Working as an Amigo at the Pilgrim Office came to be one of my favorite Camino-related experiences. In 2014, I first did this partially out of curiosity and partially because I wanted to know more about everything having to do with the Camino de Santiago. But the people I meet, experiences I have, and the positive effect this work has on me personally makes the entire effort hugely beneficial. This is a brief retelling of some of these experiences.

Five of our volunteer group were lodged in a house on the western side of the old town in Santiago. We were a good ten-minute walk from the Pilgrim Office. The location was very quiet, except for the Cathedral bells that tolled until midnight every night.

We each had private rooms with private bathrooms. The two couples among us had 'matrimonial' beds. This is what a standard full-size bed is called in Spain. I had a smaller room at the back with a single or twin-sized bed.

The house was very clean, recently renovated inside and the rear patio was completely tiled over. This is where we would come to dry out washed clothes, as there was a washing machine under the counter in the kitchen.

I went to a China store in Santiago to obtain some clothesline cord to string extra drying space. Five people require a fair amount of drying space.

However, we did come to find out that, if it was a sunny day, clothes hung out straight from the spin cycle of the washing machine would usually be completely dry in about an hour. Between the hot Spanish sun and the gentle prevailing breezes, wet clothing, linens and towels, dried very fast, usually in about one hour or so.

We developed an informal cycle of taking turns with the washing machine usually when another volunteer was working a different shift than you were. Some nights we cooked in. Having several people in the group who liked cooking helped a lot. Sadly, that does not include me.

Our sponsor, Johnnie Walker, a very generous man, had special dinners for the group along with the Dutch volunteers and the religious sisters who staffed the Camino Companions at the Pilgrim Office. It was great to share a meal with everyone together.

Back at the shared house, one of the unique things about my room is that it was at the back of the house with the sloped roof of the formal dining area below. The low end of the roof led onto the paved patio. My two windows had standard European-style, aluminum roller blinds. Typical for Europe, there were no "mosquiteros" or window screens on the windows. If you wanted cool air at night, you opened the windows and the shades.

This led to an incident on the first or second night I was there. While asleep, I felt something with four legs jump on me and walk over the bed covers. At home, I had two cats, so the sensation was not foreign to me.

I threw the bedcovers back and leapt from bed, while shouting HEY! I saw a cat fly out one of the totally open windows onto the sloped shed roof that ended just inches from the window sill. Okay, lesson learned. Good thing it was a cat and not something else, like a rat.

It was a good thing I knew how to use the roller shades. I knew that if you rolled them all the way closed, then backed off maybe two inches, you would have visual privacy, but open hundreds of tiny slotted holes for air to pass through. That was to become the only way to keep the cats out of my room whether I was away working or asleep.

I like cats, but this was not a good way to get a proper night's sleep. Still, during the time I was there, I was occasionally serenaded by one or more cats outside on the stone wall or the sloped roof just outside my windows. That is why pilgrims carry ear plugs, among other reasons.

We all enjoyed living together, working together and sharing our Camino experiences with the pilgrims we met. More significant, to me at least, were the stories that arriving pilgrims would tell us. They would share things from their private lives, things that occurred on their Caminos, and how making this journey had affected them. The general thread was that walking a Camino was a very life affecting experience for the majority of pilgrims.

29

Babbo Natale

Santiago de Compostela, Galicia, Spain

June 2014 (V)

During the second week of our two-week volunteer stint, we had a rainy day. Actually, it rained about every third day on average. This seems to be a pattern in Galicia. My late pilgrim friend Philip Wren liked to comment that, "The rain in Spain falls mainly…on Galicia." He was so right. On the other hand, that is why this region of Spain is so green and beautiful.

As the Pilgrim Office was tiny and had no room for pilgrims to wait inside under cover from the sun or rain, we all, including volunteers like me, got a proper tan, or got wet. I had walked into Santiago de Compostela from my Camino, so I had a poncho and a raincoat to wear when I worked. Many pilgrims did not have any rain protection at all.

I resorted to raiding the area souvenir shops to buy inexpensive plastic sheet ponchos for €1,00 each. After doing this a few times, a couple of the shops would give me a volume discount. They knew I was a volunteer, I was wearing the Amigo t-shirt, and they knew I was giving these away for free.

I would give them to one or more pilgrims waiting patiently in the queue and tell them to use it over themselves. I also asked them to leave the poncho in the Pilgrim Office when they were done, so I could reuse the ponchos again. Only about a quarter of the pilgrims returned these loaner ponchos. But it did not really matter. I was there to greet arriving pilgrims and to see to their needs.

On one such rainy day, I was on the street outside, Rúa do Vilar, managing the queue of waiting pilgrims. This ancient street is very narrow and closed to general vehicle traffic. After 11:00 a.m., only taxis and emergency vehicles are allowed to access this area. Still, with hundreds of waiting pilgrims each day, it could sometimes be an interesting thing when trying to get the queue of pilgrims to do anything.

This day on the street, the queue had somehow strayed from staying close up to the building and was hanging several meters out into the street. Taxis, and the odd police car on patrol could not easily get past the queue, in addition to the regular foot traffic going both directions on the street. My role was to keep the queue in place and orderly.

I approached the folks on the queue and asked them in English, and again in very basic Spanish, to please move one meter to the left, closer to the building. The queue began to slowly move.

Except, there was one group of perhaps six or seven Italian pilgrims who were busily chatting amongst themselves, while chain-smoking cigarettes, working on their smartphones, and steadfastly ignoring me. I asked them again, directly, to please move one meter to the left so vehicles and other people could get by.

Several of the men and women just stared at me. Clearly, they had no intention of being helpful and moving a meter to the left to help traffic matters.

I approached them once more, this time saying in English that surely at least one person in their group understood even a little English. Perhaps that one person could explain what I was asking them to do. No luck. Again, I got the cold stare.

"Okay I said, we can do this the easy way. The easy way is

that you politely move like everyone else." No motion.

Next, I say, "OR we can do this the hard way. I know that some of you understand me. Do you remember when you were little children and you had to be extra good for Saint Nicholas Day, or Babbo Natale would not give you any gifts? Do you remember what happens if Babbo Natale finds out you are not being polite to others?"

Now, they think I am stark crazy. While I am mostly of Italian descent, I do not speak Italian, but I do retain some cultural knowledge. I shrugged my shoulders, in a classic Italian body language motion that says 'so be it' and slide into one of the few Italian phrases I do know. "Va bene." This can mean it's good, or okay, or "whatever." It is the tone that is said with. I let it trail off. This implied something was to follow.

I walked through the portal gates into the courtyard to find my Amigo buddy Santa Brad. I found him at the head of the line instructing the next waiting pilgrims. I told him that I had a "Babbo Natale" call on the street and quickly explained these folks would not cooperate and move when I asked them to, several times. I told him they were likely just ignoring me and choosing to be indifferent to my requests.

Brad struts outside to the street, turns to where the group is still chain-smoking, chattering on and working their smartphones. He literally pulls his belly up, put his arms out in a classic Italian challenging manner and breaks into a torrent of fluid and fluent Italian.

The gist of what he said was something like: "Hey what's up, what's going on here? What's the problem?" Remember, Brad looks EXACTLY like the Saint Nicholas or Babbo Natale character that all these adults grew up knowing. He speaks Italian like a native, and even has the necessary body language down.

These folks are seeing the incarnation of Babbo Natale. You should have seen the near-immediate reaction. The group of Italian pilgrims was dumbstruck! Cigarettes simply fell from lips to the street. Jaws dropped. Conversation stopped. Phones went into pockets. They were now paying full attention. They were busted and they knew it!

When some of them looked at me, I merely shrugged my shoulders, stating that I had warned them about the easy way and the hard way. Now that they chose the hard way, they would have to convince the big guy. The looks on their faces and the immediate change in attitude was something to see. I became unable to contain myself and had to turn away before I burst out laughing.

Brad went on for a couple of minutes. But he got them to move. We had no problems with this group for the rest of the arrival and processing. But this is something that remains with me forever. The look on their faces when the character of their youth appeared in front of them in hiking boots and cargo pants to chastise them in fluent Italian was priceless.

No Way, Way!

Santiago de Compostela, Galicia, Spain

June 2014 (V)

This is another example of the wonder that resides in the souls of children and not so young people. Each day, I would walk along the queue outside, chatting with arriving and waiting pilgrims, asking them about their Caminos, where they were from, and just generally making them feel welcome. I would answer questions and provide helpful advice or directions when asked.

One morning, "Santa" Brad and I were working the line from the head of the line to the rear, outside on the street. We alternated going back and forth so the waiting pilgrims would see different people working.

In the courtyard, to one side, was a huge granite picnic table. It was perhaps two meters or nearly seven feet long and one meter or a yard wide. There were two stationary granite benches. As this table was more or less in the queue waiting to enter the office, pilgrims would sit down for perhaps ten minutes until the queue advanced and they would get up and stand once more.

On this morning, there is a group of six young college-aged women. I had chatted briefly with them and determined they were indeed students from "Minnesnowda," or Minnesota in the U.S. They used the snow-laced term as this state gets a large amount of snow each winter. The locals coined the phrase.

As we are chatting, Brad walks behind me to work further down the line or on the street. No sooner does he walk away than the girls start talking to one another. I hear acclamations of "No Way!" "No, it's simply not possible!"

Now, I KNOW what they are chatting about. They know they just saw Santa Claus in the flesh and are debating the possibility. When one of the young women acclaims, "No Way!" I jump in and state, "Way!" They look at me with confused looks. While chatting, I learn a few of the names of the women.

I told them that is indeed who they saw. I asked what they thought Santa Claus might do in the off-season when he does not need to be at the North Pole? I told them that he usually stopped by here for a while to help arriving pilgrims as it mixes things up for him. Doing the exact same thing for several millennia does get old.

Now, they are very confused. In their hearts, they WANT to believe. But their brains are fighting. I decide to sink the hook. "Would you ladies like to meet Santa directly? I can make it happen." The reaction from these women in the early 20s was like a bunch of five-year-old girls.

I walked out to the street and told Brad there was a group of women, college students from Minnesota, who think they saw Santa Claus. They were debating it when I stepped in and told him you were doing this in the off-season when the elves ran the show up north. He agreed we might have some fun. I passed the several names I had gleaned from the group.

Brad adopts his Santa strut, and approaches the group of young women. They were in rapt disbelief, blushing, giggling and just besides themselves with childlike glee. Brad starts with a "Ho, ho, ho, who thinks I am not the real thing?" Then he starts dropping names and asking who has been a good girl, a bad girl or a VERY naughty girl. Using the names that I gave him he spun a narrative that had these women blushing very deeply and cringing in front of "Santa Claus."

The woman are losing it. Brad is playing it for all it is worth. Over the years, he learned to read people, in much the same way as a fortune teller might. He can tell what people are likely thinking and can ask leading questions to elicit comments. The things the girls say, and just reply to, are providing more material for Brad to work his spell over them.

The entire event lasted perhaps ten minutes. Finally, one of the girls asked if they could do selfies with Santa. Clearly, they now believed, or thought they believed. Either way, it made everyone's day.

I stepped in and offered to play photographer using the women's smartphones or cameras. A proper good time was had by all. It would have been nice to be present when they showed those photos, and told the story of how they met the REAL Santa Claus in Santiago de Compostela.

31

Are There No Toilet Plungers in Spain!
Santiago de Compostela, Galicia, Spain

June 2014 (V)

The Pilgrim Office at Rúa do Vilar 3 was at least several hundred years old. A former home for a wealthy person, it became Church property and was later converted to use as a gift shop for the Cathedral with retail spaces rented out in the front on the street. The home proper and its courtyard were the Pilgrim Office until 2016.

Directly opposite the double gate into the courtyard is a building that was originally the coach house or stable for carriages and horses for the house. Upstairs from the stalls was a hay loft to hold feed for the winter months.

Now, this space was multi-purposed. The hayloft was made available to the Netherlands Friends of Saint James Society or "het Genootschap van Sint Jacob." This Dutch group operates a lounge or "huiskamer" primarily for the benefit of Dutch-speaking pilgrims from all over the world. Beyond the 20 million or so Netherlanders, South Africans speak a dialect of the Dutch language, and there are even some pilgrims from Indonesia who remember how to speak Dutch as this was a former Dutch colony until the Second World War.

On the ground floor were located the men's and women's bathrooms. Plumbing was installed. The stalls were tiled over. Walls, stalls, urinals and sinks were installed. Needless to say, these bathrooms got a lot of use daily.

One morning, I overheard that the toilets in the women's bathroom were not flushing properly. I entered the area when no one was there and tried to flush. It was correct, the water was not emptying from any of the toilets when the flush cycle was activated. I created a sign and closed the toilets. Per procedure, I immediately told a staff member, who then called someone to report it and, presumably, to get a plumber there to repair the problem.

The rest of that day, we used the men's toilets for both women and men. In Europe this is not at all uncommon. But it helps if someone monitors things to avoid embarrassing incidents. Fortunately, we had no problems.

The next day, the situation had not changed. The janitorial staff had come in and cleaned both bathrooms. But the women's side still was not useable.

When I arrived at 10:00 am and seeing that no plumber had yet come, I made another of my command decisions. I let the other Amigo and office staff know that I was going to look for a toilet plunger and take care of this problem myself. Clearly, waiting for the appropriate plumber person was not working.

For the next two hours, I searched every hardware store, kitchen supply store, supermarket, China store and even appliance stores in both the old town and new town sections of Santiago de Compostela for a proper toilet plunger.

This device has a long stick, about two feet long and a rubber dome or bulb on the bottom. One places the rubber dome over the clogged drain then pumps the handle up and down, in a churning motion, to create overpressure to force a clog down the pipe and permit a clogged drain or toilet to work.

I knew what I was looking for. When I would go to a proper ferretería or hardware store and use my Google Translator to ask for a toilet plunger or "émbolo higiénico" (in Spanish), I received one of three replies:

- We do not carry such a thing,

- I have never heard of such a thing, or

- Let me show you…

In the latter case, the proprietor would always take me to the kitchen section and show me a sink-sized plunger. It was conceptually the same thing, but was in no way large enough for what I had in mind.

Finally, I gave up. I bought a sink plunger and a pair of rubber gloves. It might not be pretty, but it might just work.

Fortunately, in my absence, the others kept anyone from using the women's bathrooms. Conditions were not as bad as they could have been. I was dealing with largely clear water and only a little bit of toilet tissue. After double checking that the drains were still clogged, I put my gloves on and got busy.

This attracted a stream of people who were frankly very curious as to what I was doing. I worked at it for perhaps 45 minutes before I finally concluded that the problem was not the individual toilets, but the common drain they used. I was exhausted.

This was now day two of the toilet outage and no workers had yet appeared. My shift ended at 3:00 pm and no one had yet come.

The next day, day three of the toilet outage I arrived at 10:00 am to see a large hole in the middle of the courtyard, perhaps five meters in front of the toilet area. This hole was about a meter deep, and a meter square. There were four men in worker's uniforms at the hole, discussing the situation in Spanish.

At the bottom of the hole was a terra cotta drain pipe about

4 inches in diameter. Back home, we would call this type of pipe Orangeburg pipe. It was only extruded and fired clay. In my recollection, it has not been used for sewerage drains for about 50 years. Clearly, this piping was likely several hundred years old. Anyway, the workers appeared to be discussing just how big this project might be.

All day long the workers labored on this hole and the pipe. In the end, they cut a section of pipe to create two clean-cut ends. Over this they attached a rubber and stainless-steel / inox collar or patch. The patch connected both parts of the pipe with a rubber tube of the proper diameter, and fastened in place with very large clamps tightened with a screwdriver. The end result looks like the radiator hose on an automobile engine, albeit larger in diameter.

It was not until very late on day three of this saga that the hole was finally filled in and the paving stones replaced. But and I hasten to add, in my experience this sort of repair is considered a patch and is temporary. Then again, what about the men's bathrooms? Had they even taken a look at that common drain. No!

This brought to mind several conclusory observations on my part:

- If it is not broken yet, do not fix it,

- Everything broken will get repaired…eventually, and

- Apparently, toilets in Spain never get stopped up.

Some years later, in 2018, I did find a proper plunger in a large do-it-yourself hardware store outside Santiago de Compostela. But, by then of course, we had already moved into a newly renovated Pilgrim Office location with all new plumbing. Still, one does wonder.

Spain Has NO Bad Wine

Santiago de Compostela, Galicia, Spain

June 2014 (V)

I mentioned previously that living in the shared Amigo house we sometimes cooked in and had a proper meal prepared by someone who could actually cook a healthy meal. On one of these occasions, I offered to supply the wine. We had been having a running conversation about having good wine in Spain. There was general agreement that Spain only made good wine.

Deciding to put that proposition to a test at that evening's meal, I went to a local supermarket after my shift in the Pilgrim Office to buy wine. As I was looking over the offerings at the rear of the store, I had an inspiration. I would arrange a wine tasting.

I found a selection of wine from a single vineyard in La Rioja. I bought three bottles: a white wine, a rosé, and a red. I do not remember the varietals, but they were all local types of wine. After buying the wine, I removed the price labels and brought the wine to the shared house. The white and rosé went into the refrigerator. The red was placed on the dining table.

As we gathered for the evening meal, I announced that I had supplied the wine as promised, but was going to use the opportunity to prove my point that Spain did not produce bad wine. We were to start with the cold white wine before dinner, enjoy the rosé with our light summer meal, then follow with cheese, fruit and the red wine for dessert.

We dined, had a pleasant time, and enjoyed opening each bottle of wine and sharing our opinions on the relative merits of each bottle. Everyone enjoyed each bottle of wine to varying degrees. Each of us had a preference. However, and in my opinion, all three of these wines were very drinkable. I had enjoyed better wine and worse wine, but as table wines, all three of these bottles were very acceptable.

Once the third bottle of wine was consumed, and all present were feeling jolly, I decided to spring my private surprise. Explaining that deciding if a wine was good or bad was in part a value proposition. In other words, the lower the price of the bottle of wine, the more likely someone is likely to find merit or value in their choice. Conversely, the more expensive a bottle of wine is, the greater the value one expects, and usually is more critical in judging the value of the expensive bottle of wine.

We discussed each bottle of wine and I asked each person if they would pay for this at home and how much they thought the price might be at home. Everyone joined in and agreed that these wines might sell for somewhere in a range of USD 7 to 10 dollars (€ 6 to 8).

I removed the store receipt from my pocket and laid it out on the table. Each bottle of wine had cost less than € 2,00 ($ 2.20). In fact, two of the three were about €1,80 (about $ 2.00). The others were shocked. But I proved my point. Spanish vineyards offer a wide variety of quality table wines at incredibly good price points.

On the other hand, after three bottles of wine and a proper meal, everyone was in a very agreeable mood anyway.

33

Meeting the Shadow Pilgrim

Santiago de Compostela, Galicia, Spain

June 2014 (V)

The old city of Santiago de Compostela is full of very interesting places to see and there is a lot to learn. The Cathedral is about 900 years old. As the Cathedral was developed over the years, the city grew up around it. This was the general pattern in most large European towns and cities. It was a variant of the saying "Build it, and they will come."

Once the foundations for the Cathedral were placed around 1075 AD, additional guildsmen, skilled workers to build the Cathedral, then tradesmen to sell them things followed. In much of Europe, the first homes were built with wood, or partially with wood. But in Galicia, and indeed in the area of Santiago de Compostela, quarrying granite has been a local industry since humans first inhabited this place. Most of the Cathedral was built of granite.

The nooks and crannies of this huge building provide many interesting places to visit and photograph. The architecture is incredible.

However, there is also mystery and legend at play here. While thinking about how to approach telling this story from my perspective, I also researched what others have said about this phenomenon. The result was quite a body of varied but complementary stories… Anyway, here is my telling of the thing.

One night, a fellow volunteer asked me if I had met the ghost of Saint James yet. Clearly, I had not. He told me to meet him at the top of the stairs from Praza das Praterías, on the South side of the Cathedral at 9:45 pm.

In Spain in July, it does not get fully dark in the summer until after 10:00 pm. But I met my colleague there as agreed. We went for a drink at one of the several cafes along one side of the adjacent Plaza Quintana. I recall it was the one on the far end of the row of cafes.

Sitting outside, it was finally getting dark and the outdoor lights were all on. He told me to look at the Cathedral. Specifically, he told me to look carefully to the right of the now-closed, door to the Cathedral gift shop, in the corner of the Cathedral.

This is what I saw… What do you think?

I was told it was the ghost of Santiago. As I mentioned, there are several explanations for this phenomenon. But, seeing is believing. First, the alternative legends, there are least four versions of the origin of this apparition:

The first version (Wandering Souls) relates to the past use of Plaza Quintana. This large flat area is between the east side of the Cathedral and the west wall of the convent of the Benedictine sisters. Plaza Quintana is split into two levels. One is higher up a broad stairway popular today as a viewing place for the many shows and concerts staged in this large open plaza. The plaza is next to the cathedral and is divided into two levels separated by a staircase that splits its surface in two. The area at the highest elevation is called Quintana de Vivos. This is something akin to "place of the living." The flat plaza at the bottom of these stairs, and adjacent to the east side of the Cathedral is called Quintana de Mortos, or something like "place of the dead." In addition, the lower part of the plaza was at one time a public cemetery. Many people believe the shadow of the pilgrim is a manifestation of the wandering soul of some of those who rested there.

The second explanation (Unrighteous Death) has to do with one of the more unpleasant historical periods in the history of the Catholic Church. Once the Moors were forced out of Spain in 1492, Church and local authorities turned on the local population to expunge anyone who was not a devout Catholic. This dark period of history was the Spanish Inquisition. During this period, a lot of nasty and dark activities occurred all over Spain, even in Santiago de Compostela. In the context of our shadow pilgrim, some say that the shadow belongs to the soul of some unhappy person who was burned at the stake by inquisitorial judgment.

A third version (another Wandering Soul) to explain the apparition of the Shadow Pilgrim is that the shadow belongs to the soul of Leónard du Revenant, a 15th century French pilgrim. This man was condemned to travel to Santiago to purge himself of the murder of his father (León de Cornu), whom he killed to inherit his fortune. Along the way, as he passed through Navarre, the Frenchman met an innkeeper whom he tried to seduce. She rejected him, and this caused him to fight with the girl's boyfriend. Leónard, in revenge, stalked the young woman, assaulting her and later killing the couple. On his arrival in Santiago, León de Cornu appeared to him, announcing that his death was purged but not that of the other two innocents. Thus, Leónard would have to wait in the Cathedral for their souls to appear before he could be forgiven. Hence, every night, Leónard's shadow appears impassively waiting for the souls of the bride and groom whom he murdered.

The fourth version (Unrequited Love) of the reason for the Shadow Pilgrim apparition I found was the legend of the priest and the nun. Legend has it that a priest from the Cathedral and a nun from a convent on the other side of the square maintained a secret romance. The priest, tired of having to hide his love, proposed to his lover to flee from Santiago away from censored glances. The priest disguised himself as a pilgrim to not attract attention. The story goes that he waited behind the Cathedral for the nun for hours, but she never appeared. In this legend, the Shadow Pilgrim is the disguised priest. He never resigned himself to losing his beloved and returns every night to wait for her, forever.

Lastly, the version that was told to me is that this is the ghost of Santiago Peregrino, Saint James dressed in his pilgrim attire with staff. He appears every night to watch over pilgrims partying next door at the several cafes. Okay, it works for me. Call it at least five reasons for the apparition.

It is not strange that a city with the extensive history of

Santiago and the multitude of people who have walked its streets, is an inexhaustible source of legends, tales and myths. The silhouette that is projected daily on one of the facades of the Cathedral appears to all to be that of a pilgrim dressed in a wide-brimmed hat, walking stick, gourd (for water) and cape. All traditional garb for the well-dressed pilgrim of the Middle Ages.

Personally, I like all of the explanations. Over the decades, this apparition has become one of the most celebrated things to see each night in Santiago. It is still amazing whenever I ask newly arriving pilgrims if they have met the Shadow Pilgrim yet. Most everyone says no. It provides a nice ice breaker for conversation.

My First Quemada
Santiago de Compostela, Galicia, Spain

June 2014 (V)

During the second week of my first volunteer stint at the Pilgrim Office in Santiago our very kind host, Mr. Johnnie Walker, arranged for a group dinner for all the volunteers working that week. He included the six of us American volunteers, the two Dutch volunteers staffing their 'Huiskamer' lounge for Dutch speakers, the religious sisters running the Camino Companions welcoming and counseling service, and one or two English-speaking priests present in Santiago, and we were working with Johnnie's Camino Chaplaincy.

In all, I recall there were ten or twelve of us. A restaurant was arranged that could provide a large banquet-sized round table for all of us. As was usually the case whenever Johnnie Walker arranged a meal for us, the food was wonderful and plentiful.

I was also beginning to like the Spanish custom of a 'bottomless' wine glass. It is similar in concept to free refills of soft drinks in the U.S. But in Spain, they take it to an entirely new level. You pay for soft drink refills, but in a banquet setting, the wine refills just keep coming. Viva España!

I need to digress a bit here to explain what a Quemada is. First, it is pronounced (kay-MA-da). The word is also sometimes spelled "Queimada." The word "quemada" or "queimada" means "burned." I will use the spelling quemada here.

The Quemada is a Galician ritual to ward off evil spirits. It is believed to be an ancient Celtic tradition passed down through the ages. It is intended to cast out demons and bad spirits through an incantation and a witches' brew made of orujo.

The drink is prepared in a clay pot which represents the earth. Galician aguardiente de orujo, a distilled brandy with **extremely** high alcohol content, represents water (or the tears of Mother Nature) and becomes the base of this drink. The aguardiente de orujo is mixed with herbs or coffee, sugar, lemon peel, and coffee beans.

A flame is ignited over the cauldron / pot and the alcohol begins to burn, representing light. Sugar is scooped from the bottom of the clay pot, creating a beautiful cascade of blue fire as it caramelizes. At the end of the ceremony, when the flames subside, a hot, tan colored beverage is left to be ladled into clay cups.

Now I need to explain what Orujo is…

Orujo is a pomace brandy (a liquor obtained from the distillation of the solid remains after pressing of the grape) from northern Spain. It is a transparent spirit with an alcohol content over 50% (100° proof). Its name comes from the expression "aguardiente de orujo" (pomace spirit).

Grape pomace has been used in other cultures to produce similar pomace brandies (such as grappa, orujo, or ouzo). The distilling process takes six hours or more. The copper stills used by Galicians for centuries are in some cases hundreds of years old. The orujo produced by this distillation is a colorless liquor, while orujo envejecido or "aged orujo" is amber in color. The aged variety is fermented and distilled the same way, but is then poured into oak barrels to age for at least two years. Remember, the fresh, unaged variety is 100 proof. One can only guess at how much alcohol the two-year old stuff has…

From orujo, Galicians traditionally make the ceremonial drink called quemada, in which bits of lemon peel, sugar and ground coffee are put into a clay cauldron / pot or a hollow pumpkin when available. Then the orujo is poured on top and the pot is lit on fire until the flame turns blue.

Okay, back to the ritual…

As the flames rise from the burning sugar, an incantation is chanted, usually in Spanish. But it is also done in Gallego, the local dialect in Galicia. The incantation or spell is actually a poem called "conxuro" (con-SHU-roh). It is said to protect the soul from evil spirits that are nearby. Notably, it includes such significant lines as:

"…With this bellows I will pump the flames of this fire which looks like from Hell, and witches will flee, straddling their brooms… and when this beverage goes down our throats, we will get free of the evil of our soul and of any charm.

Forces of air, earth, sea and fire, to you I make this call: if it is truth that you have more power than human people, here and now, make the spirits of the friends who are outside, take part with us in this quemada …"

Legend says that the first sip of the Quemada purifies the soul by banishing out evil spirits, the second cleans the mind of prejudices, and the third gives rise to passion. I think that the fourth sip usually results in hitting the floor…

In my research, I came across a statement that some say that this 'tradition' was only established in the 1950's when an artisan named Tito Freire designed the ceramic pot and serving bowls that are typically used for this ceremony. But ancient legends tend to disprove that claim. Accounts from history include using a hollow gourd or pumpkin to mix the concoction.

The spell that is widely used today was written by Mariano Marcos Abalo in the 1960s. This might add to speculation that the Quemada is not as old a tradition as you might think. However, many Celtic traditions are oral traditions, so would not have been written down and they adapted these rituals over the centuries. Moreover, and as my research indicated, as Christianity was introduced and spread, the incantation and spells started to include Christian elements and words.

Okay, now we return to our convivial meal…

Imagine, it is night time, well – the room is darkened – you have enjoyed a wonderful, hearty meal of traditional Galician dishes. It really was a meal for the record books. Anticipation is felt as you gather around. Now is the time for the Quemada.

The Quemada glazed ceramic cauldron or pot, represents Mother Earth. It is filled with the potion of orujo, to represent the element of water and the tears of Mother Earth. To then make them bittersweet like many tears, coffee beans, lemon peel and sugar are added.

The master of ceremonies, in his case a waiter from the restaurant, plays the role of a Druid priest. He takes the long-handled ladle, fills it with the potion, and sets the contents on fire, transforming it to represent the element of light.

Slowly moving the ladle back down to the potion in the clay pot and stirring the liquor from the bottom, the fumes coming off this potion burn brightly. A bright blue flame dances on top of the liquid. The ladle is lifted high above the clay pot spilling the liquid back into the pot, only to be dipped back in, again and again. This creates a fountain effect of blue and amber burning liquid that hypnotizes as the spell is read aloud.

One of the volunteers reads the ritual incantation – in English – the flames danced in the cauldron / pot. We are all listening to the incantation. It takes some ten minutes. The incantation is very long, interesting and at times engrossing, but long.

At the close of the incantation, the fiery blend in the

cauldron is scooped using the ladle into each of the ceramic mugs surrounding the Quemada. Once everyone has a flaming ceramic cup of this fire water, we are told to blow the flame out and to sip the liquor.

The ceramic mug is warm to the touch as I raise it to my lips. I take a healthy sip – more of a swig – short of doing a shot. YIKES! No one warned me beforehand that orujo was 100 proof, or more. I only learned that later, when researching this.

Without thinking, my mouth just spewed the mouthful of orujo across the table. This prompted the priest sitting next to me to exclaim, NO ONE light a match! I might have been a fire breather.

Fortunately, I did not burn the restaurant down. However, everyone had a good laugh at my expense.

Since that time, I have attended several other Quemada ceremonies in and around Santiago. NOW, I know that a sip means to wet your lips, and NO MORE – at least until the fire water cools down and you can assess your options, like having a glass of water and a fire extinguisher nearby.

Dirt Naps!

Northern Portugal, after Porto

May 2015 (P)

My third Camino was an effort to change things a bit by trying another popular route. I opted to walk the Portuguese Camino from Porto to Santiago de Compostela via the central route. For those walking all the way from Lisbon on the traditional route used long ago by King Ferdinand and Queen Isabella of Spain, the route enters Porto, then continues on to Santiago. I would do the final segment, some 250 kilometers over about ten days.

As was becoming my standard approach to a Camino, in my third consecutive year, I booked transportation into Lisbon with a return from Lisbon. Later, after my Camino and some social time at Santiago, I would take a train from Santiago de Compostela to La Coruña, then a taxi to the airport, there to take a flight to Lisbon to connect back to my home. This was the easy bit.

To me, the ten days walking from Porto to Santiago was comparable in difficulty as the final segment of the Camino Francés from Sarria to Santiago. The people are very helpful and more Portuguese speak at least some English than is the case in Spain. Several Portuguese I met along the way told me this was because all their prime-time evening television is native English language programming from the U.K, U.S., Canada or

Australia, and it is all shown with Portuguese subtitles. All similar programming in Spain is dubbed into Spanish, without subtitles.

I chose to depart Porto at the end of April and walked through the early part of May. Most days were very mild and sunny, with very little rain. My reserved lodgings were all very good and I was having a positive Camino experience. While I may not have formed a formal Camino family at the beginning as is usually the case on the Camino Francés, I did come upon many very nice and friendly pilgrims each day.

It is my preference to walk a solo Camino, as two or more pilgrims can usually only walk as fast as the slowest person. My walking speed varies with my mood, energy level, the weather, and who I happen to be walking with. Over time, and through experience, I have learned that I walk a three kilometer per hour pace on uphill segments, four kilometers per hour on level to rolling terrain, and a five kilometer per hour pace on downhill segments. For planning purposes each morning, I generally look at the distance to be covered, in kilometers, divide by four, and round up to the next whole number to get a fairly accurate estimate of my planned arrival time at the day's destination.

I mentioned that most days were sunny and mild. Temperatures were in the mid 20s (Celsius) or mid to upper 70s (Fahrenheit). The skies were crystal blue, with nary a cloud in the sky. There was a gentle breeze. Walking along for hours on end I did not feel thirsty, nor do I recall perspiring. I do recall that I was wearing a sun hat.

One late morning I am walking along, pole, step, pole, step. The next moment I am on one knee on the ground, wondering what the heck just happened. It was as though someone had flipped a switch and turned me off. For a moment I was very confused. I got back to my feet, stepped into the shade of a tree and sat down. Though not feeling especially thirsty or light headed, I drank a full half-liter of water. After a five-minute rest, I started out again, feeling fine.

Several hours later, that afternoon, after a lunch break, complete with my typical ham and cheese bocadillo (sandwich), and topping off my water supplies, I am once again walking on a Camino path. As I walk alone, there is no one near me. Again, place the pole, step, place the pole, step. Once more I suddenly find myself on the same knee, my system having been turned off, again.

Now I am growing a little concerned. Two near-dirt naps in one day. I feel fine. I am not running a fever. I have no stomach ailments. The weather is great and I have no aches and pains.

The good news is that my destination for the day is near. I get to my lodgings, go through the regular routine of shower, put on clean clothes, hand wash, hang to dry, and roam about the town for something to eat. All the while, I am wondering what the heck could have caused me to just fold like a marionette with its strings cut, out of the blue. I was conscious and walking one moment, and on my knees the next. Okay, the next day, I headed out again, with plenty of water and snacks, some with salt. I was beginning to wonder about an electrolyte shortage. I had a banana for breakfast and was carrying an orange for later consumption. These are both potassium-rich foods that are excellent for restoring low blood salts or electrolytes.

In mid-morning, I stopped at a café for coffee and a type of tortilla. This being Portugal, it was not quite the same as in Spain. In Spain, tortilla is a sort of quiche pie made of flaked potatoes and egg in a light pastry shell. I took the opportunity to eat my orange as well.

Around 1:30 pm in the afternoon, walking along an ancient Roman road, under clear blue sky, I am content, thinking of nothing in particular. Pole, step, pole, step… When all of a sudden, I awake face-down with my arm in front of my face, which is in the dirt. My wire-frame eyeglasses are all mangled and a lens has popped out.

I am not amused! Three dirt naps in two days. Clearly there is something wrong that I cannot identify.

I get to my knees, actually on my hands and knees, locate the missing eyeglass lens, and gradually managed to stand up. Into the shade I went. Fortunately, I carry a spare pair of eyeglasses so that swap was made and the damaged pieces from the mangled pair and the lens saved in the spare pair case.

Now I am worried. I am not even out of Portugal yet. With a week or more to complete to get to Santiago I am assessing my situation.

My initial assessment is that the symptoms most nearly resemble dehydration. This can occur even in mild weather if you do not hydrate and do not replenish electrolytes lost through perspiration. I knew it could occur even if one did not feel prostrated from intense heat or sunlight.

I forced myself to drink a full liter of water and then proceeded to walk carefully to the next destination. There, I found bottled water, and a pharmacy that carried a rehydration powder, nominally for use with babies having diarrhea. The good news is that I was able to obtain it in a variety of fruit flavors.

Overnight, I went lightly on alcohol consumption and tried to eat foods that contained salts. These three incidents seriously impressed on me the critical need to preemptively hydrate, even if I did not feel thirsty.

My hydration plan emerged. I would force myself to consume one-half liter of water every hour even if I did not feel thirsty. Every third drink, or every third hour, would be a mixed rehydration mix powder. Again, I would do this whether I felt I needed it or not.

Over the course of a six-hour walking day, I would have three liters of water, with one of those liters being two half-liter rehydration drinks. Now, I am not a sports therapist, doctor, nurse, or an exercise professional. I just applied what I knew from basic research and life experience.

Whatever the reason, it worked. I had no further dirt nap episodes all the way to my arrival at Santiago de Compostela, ten days after departing Porto.

The Aftermath

On my return home, I went to my doctor who put me through a battery of tests to check my cardiac health, brain health, and everything else they could think of. The official medical diagnosis then in 2015, was probably dehydration caused by stupidity. That is what my personal doctor actually told me. I have no idea what he actually noted in my medical records.

Fast Forward

Four years later in 2019, I was making plans to do another Camino. This time on the Primitivo. I had been having some rare and widely distributed episodes of light-headedness. I had my annual physical, as I usually do before Camino season. The doctor could not find anything conclusive. However, he did come up with an interesting hypothesis.

In April 2005, I had a bariatric lap band installed on my stomach to lose a lot of weight. I was morbidly obese. I did lose about 45 kilos or around 100 pounds. Since then, I had been supplementing my daily diet with powdered protein drinks, as liquids were easiest to pass through the hour-glass-shaped stomach I had.

One of the things that made the lap band work is that it applies gentle pressure against the vagus nerve. This is a major nerve system that runs from one's brain to the gut. It is this nerve that, when pressed by a fully stuffed stomach, like after a huge meal, tells the brain to shunt blood to the stomach muscle to assist with digestion. In turn, the brain sends blood from other regions of the body, like the head to the stomach. The resulting blood pressure drop in the head is what produces the light-headedness that causes a lot of people to nap after consuming a huge meal.

Having a bariatric band press lightly against this important nerve means that the brain is always told that you are full. This explains why I never again had hunger pangs after the band was installed. As a result, my doctor's hypothesis was that I needed to see my gastroenterologist to have the lap-band further evaluated to see if this might not be a proximate cause of my recent light-headedness.

Long story shortened. The gastroenterologist had a barium swallow diagnostic test done on me. He determined that the silicone bariatric band had somehow slipped into misalignment, and had been pressing harder on the vagus nerve. This was telling my brain to send blood to the stomach to aid indigestion, when no such redistribution was needed. The adjustment tube that allowed saline solution to be added or removed to adjust the band was also broken off.

In a flash, it now made perfect sense. Back in 2015, the lap-band was likely pressing on the vagus nerve telling my brain to send more blood to the stomach. This reduced the blood pressure to my brain, This, in-turn, caused the dirt naps on my Camino from Porto to Santiago in 2015.

I was told not to undertake a 2019 Camino, and I cancelled my plans, opting to put in another two weeks volunteer work at the Pilgrim Office during May 2019.

My bariatric lap band was surgically removed in June 2019. Hopefully, that ends this problem. We will find out the next time I walk a Camino.

36

"Dominick," Part Two

Santiago de Compostela, Galicia, Spain

July 2015 (V)

I first introduced the very intriguing fellow named Dominick from the Alsace-Lorraine region of France after my first Camino in 2013. Little did I know then that our paths would cross again.

Think about it. Of all the hundreds of thousands of pilgrims who walk to Santiago de Compostela each year, and the millions over the years, what are the odds that you will just bump into someone you met previously as a one-off meeting? Let's just agree for the telling of this story that the odds are really small.

In July of 2015, I was once again working as a volunteer at the Pilgrim Office in Santiago de Compostela. This year, however, I was staying for a full month. My annual Camino had been done on a previous trip in April – May, and I returned directly to Santiago for this volunteer work. The Pilgrim Office was still located in the old pazo (town house) at Rúa do Vilar 3. Arriving pilgrims still queued in a single line around the courtyard and out onto the street. My duties were pretty much as they were last summer. However, the plumbing worked much better this year.

One morning, I was asked to sit at the small table opposite the counter where pilgrims were being interviewed for their Compostelas to sell the cardboard tubes called tubos. Pilgrims could choose to buy one of these for €2,00 to roll up their Compostelas and Certificates of Distance to protect them in transit. This is actually a very good idea as the paper documents will crinkle, crease and tear if not protected in transit. Rolling the documents into a tube is the best method, as the thick cardboard tube provides optimal protection.

Anyway, my job was to sit at this table and offer tubos for sale. Pilgrims would produce cash and I would hand over a tube. Generally, it was my practice to offer to roll the pilgrim's documents to place into the tube. Over the days I did this, I found that many pilgrims did not have the cleanest hands and my offer was intended to protect the documents. I did manage to develop a technique with a bit of a flourish and I also showed each pilgrim how to easily remove the rolled-up documents from the tube when they got home without tearing anything. Believe it or not, there is a proper way to do this.

One morning, here I am, sitting at a small table rolling many of these documents to slide into tubes I am selling. I have a carton of tubos and a cash box. Over the days, I have gotten quite good at this and I have a rhythm going.

I just happened to glance up to look at the backs of the pilgrims standing at the counter being interviewed. Directly in front of me, at the last counter position, is a tall man all dressed in black and wearing a safety lime-yellow reflective vest with tiny LED blinking lights all over it. The lights are twinkling like a Christmas tree. Then the man turns to speak with his colleague.

It is Dominick, again! He is standing there, right in front of me more than two years after I first met him. Except this time, he is all decked out in his brightly colored blinky light safety vest.

I secured the cash box, got up and crossed the two meters space while exclaiming, "Dominick! Como ça va?" (Not correct

French, but colloquially used). He turns, then recognizes me. Here are two grown men, man-hugging and shaking hands. I think he was as surprised to see me as I was him.

After we exchange greetings, I ask him how is doing… fine… Did he walk from Strasbourg again? Yes. WOW! What is he doing walking yet again? His answer is priceless.

"When I first met you, I told you that I was walking in part to thank God for healing me well enough to do my first Camino. But I was also asking for a miracle to cure me further. It occurred to me that He might have been busy or had a lot on His hands back then… so I decided to do it again, hoping He might pay attention this time…"

What faith this man had! Having recovered from a stroke and only managing to half walk, half drag himself some 1,500 kilometers from his home to get here. And he did it TWICE in three years. And I was worried about three little dirt naps in Portugal.

That Damn Train Station

Santiago de Compostela, Galicia, Spain

July 2015 (V)

When I worked as an Amigo volunteer at the Pilgrim Office in 2014, my fellow volunteers and I were housed in a private home located in a quiet neighborhood west of the Cathedral. For 2015, things changed. The Pilgrim Office had rented several large flats around the newer part of Santiago de Compostela. From September to May, these flats were occupied by university students. During the summer months, when the university was more or less closed, the Pilgrim Office rented them to house volunteers like us.

The apartment I was assigned to was located on the third floor, in an eight-floor modern building at the bottom of Rúa do Hórreo just above the Santiago de Compostela train station. Our flat overlooked the train station. The location was very convenient, about a 15-minute walk to the Pilgrim Office. Everything we might need; supermarket, cafes, restaurants, hardware store, and other assorted shops were all located on the way to and from work.

The flat was very large. It had four private bedrooms, some with two twin beds and one with a single 'matrimonial' or full-sized bed. We had a full kitchen with a washing machine, two full bathrooms, a large living room and dining room, as well as a glassed-in sun porch facing south. This porch had a clothes line that was excellent for drying clothes. You could hang wet clothes from the washing machine and they would be dry in an hour or so if it was a sunny day.

There was only one downside to this entire arrangement. The adjacent train station had a public address system that announced the arrival and departure of EVERY train from 6:00 am to 12:00 midnight. The volume was loud and it carried. Even though we were several hundred meters away and above the train station, we heard everything.

The flat was not air conditioned, so all ventilation came from having the windows open to the outside. The sun porch, living room and the two bedrooms on the south side of the flat were serenaded 18-hours daily by the alert sound then the announcements in Spanish, regarding arriving and departing trains.

This was all fine, unless you wanted to go to sleep before midnight or rise later than 6:00 am. It added 'local color' to the experience.

Meeting the Jazzman

Santiago de Compostela, Galicia, Spain

July 2015 (V)

Every city in the world has colorful local characters. Many cities with street performers or 'buskers' as they are called across Europe, have a wide range of performance types and quality. Some of these street performers are comically bad while others are surprisingly good.

Santiago de Compostela is a compact city. The old city attracts millions of tourists and hundreds of thousands of pilgrims each year. In my experience, it offers a very wide variety of street performers. From vocal performances, to traditional wind and horn instruments, classic guitar, harps, Swiss horns, Galician bag pipes, and that is only the music.

There are puppet shows, fire breathers, jugglers and pantomime artists, too. Then, there are the craftsmen, making jewelry and leather items as well as the street artists doing caricature work, portraits and antique photography. There is something for everyone.

On my previous trips to Santiago, either after arriving off a Camino or when I was there as a volunteer, I liked to go la Plaza Quintana when I had time. In the afternoon or early evening, one of my favorite things was to sit at one of the many outdoor cafes and watch the people. It was usually very entertaining.

Frequently, I was lucky enough to be there when a fellow

wearing a black balaclava hiding his face, a Panama hat and a faux cigarette hanging from his lips, would sit on a folding metal chair and play jazz guitar. I am not talking about just playing guitar. This guy was very, very good. I cannot carry a tune in a pail, nor play any musical instruments. But I know good music when I hear it.

Both in 2013 and 2014, I was thrilled to hear this fellow when I was there. In 2015, I decided to approach him and to buy the self-produced CDs he was selling. At that time, he had five CDs recorded. I bought them all.

I introduced myself and learned his English was far better than my developing Spanish. After exchanging pleasantries, I asked him about his guitar playing. He told me that he was called The Jazzman of Santiago because he was formerly a professional jazz musician. Originally from Ecuador, he used to play with Carlos Santana, the world-famous Latin-American jazz musician from the U.S. Go figure! It just goes to prove that you NEVER know who or what you will meet in Santiago de Compostela.

We had a very nice conversation. I told him, honestly, that after the whole pilgrim thing and the Botafumeiro, he was one of the main reasons I came to Santiago. I truly appreciated his music and would now have his CDs to listen to when I was home. In fact, I have them installed on my iPhone now, even the Christmas album.

They Told Me There Would Be Pilgrims

Camino de Madrid, before Segovia, Spain

April 2016 (P)

Okay, another year, another Camino route. This time, I decided to walk from Madrid on the Camino de Madrid. Interestingly enough, this is not one of the original Camino routes from the Middle Ages. It is a fairly modern invention intended to collect pilgrims from the Madrid area, and from other smaller pilgrim routes in the southern parts of Spain and to channel them north.

Historically, the Iberian Peninsula was comprised of many independent smaller kingdoms. Modern Spain and Portugal as we now know them did not emerge until after the Moors were driven from Iberia in 1492. After then, a unified Spanish state began to emerge.

As early as the middle of the ninth century, mid-800s AD, several pilgrimage routes developed coming from northern Europe beyond the Pyrenees. The Camino Francés was among the first routes developed, and even today, forms a spine or backbone of sorts for many routes joining it from all directions of the compass, on its way to Santiago de Compostela. Other very old and traditional routes, like the Portuguese, Aragonés, and Primitivo routes, for example, existed from the beginnings of the Camino de Santiago.

However, the Camino de Madrid is a different thing. The first half or more of the route starts in Madrid and ends at Sahagún where it flows into the second half of the Camino Francés, and onward to Santiago de Compostela. Sahagún is about one day east from León. The route is nominally about 320 kilometers long from Madrid to Sahagún. It takes about two weeks, until you intersect the Camino Francés at Sahagún to arrive at Santiago de Compostela.

The route is almost exclusively on footpaths and along Cañadas (historic drove roads for cattle) and rarely on tarmac roads. These Cañadas were used for hundreds of years by cattle ranchers to move cattle from summer to winter pastures and to market.

For the first 100 kilometers, the route climbs the foothills of the Sierra de Guadarrama. Crossing the Sierra includes a climb of 650m in 8 km to the Puerto de Fuenfría followed by a gradual descent to Segovia, almost all in endless pine forest.

Beyond Segovia, the terrain is rolling and near flat. The route follows the valleys of the rivers Eresma and Voltoya to the river Duero, an area of low rolling terrain with pine forests interspersed with open farm and grazing land. Past the River Duero to Sahagún is the Tierra de Campos, typical mostly flat dry Meseta with a lot of grain farming separated by ravines surrounding villages sited on road spurs. On arriving at Sahagún, one simply turns left, to the west, and continues on with the rest of the Camino Francés pilgrims all the way into Santiago de Compostela.

My story starts during the early part of April 2016. I flew into Spain and got a hotel for a couple of nights to acclimate as is my practice. My new credencial got its first sello at the Church of Santiago and Saint John the Baptist, the traditional starting place for this Camino.

Based on research, and as I do not like exiting large cities via either gritty city areas or industrial belts, I usually use public transportation to skip over these non-inspirational parts. I know, some will say this makes me not a real pilgrim. It is my Camino and this is how I do it. My first day out consisted of a train ride to Tres Cantos. I walked a full day from there. I did not meet another pilgrim on that first day – no one. I arrived at my first night's stopping place, and again found no pilgrims.

The second, third, and fourth days were pretty much the same. I stayed overnight at Colemenar Viejo, Manzanares el Real, then at Cercedilla, before making it to Segovia. On the second and third day, I did encounter a handful of local day hikers and a few local cyclists but no pilgrims headed for Santiago. On the fourth day, when I ended up at Segovia, I found myself walking with the ONLY real pilgrim I encountered in four or more days.

Originally from Germany and then living on a farm in Ireland, Brigit was convinced by her friends to walk the Camino de Santiago, and that this route would be the best as her first-ever Camino. As this was my fourth go at this Camino stuff, I patiently explained to Brigit that, in my opinion, her friends were perhaps playing a colossal joke on her. I knew from my research that this route carries relatively few pilgrims even during the peak season. We were on the front-end of the season. But my first four days certainly bore out the research. I expected relative solitude, but this was ridiculous.

Brigit was in her late 20s and having a break from her farm work. Her expectation was that she would meet other younger pilgrims, especially German pilgrims, as her friends all recounted from their Caminos. The only actual pilgrim she had yet met – me – was likely old enough to be her grandfather.

We were walking towards Segovia when I explained to Brigit that, while this was a less than stellar start to her first

Camino, I could offer some suggestions that might improve her experience. I knew that the high-speed AVE trains ran through Segovia up to León. I laid out an alternative plan for Brigit.

I suggested that she walk into Segovia with me, and take a morning train the next morning to jump ahead to León. There, she would have no problems obtaining an albergue or other lodging. As this was also nominally the halfway point on the Camino Francés, she would definitely meet other pilgrims including many her own age and certainly many German pilgrims. I recall actually promising her this would be the case.

In addition, I explained that even if she did continue on the Madrid route, she would connect to the Camino Francés at Sahagún, just east of León, then walk into León. All she was doing was leapfrogging ahead by about a week or so. I went on to explain that if she was interested in the Compostela she only had to document walking the final segment, from Sarria with at least two sellos per day, and that on that route, this was a very easy thing to do.

Brigit accepted my idea. We continued our long day's walk into Segovia. I went to my hotel, and she to hers. We met for a meal, and set a time to meet the next morning. I would see her to the train station.

Well, we did see some folks at Segovia that might have been pilgrims, but it was not like being at Burgos, León, or Ponferrada on the Francés where it seems every third person you see is a pilgrim.

When I returned to my hotel room and logged into my e-mail there were a flood of messages from home. It seems that our home in Virginia, that had been on the market to sell for seven months since we moved south to Florida, had a real and serious buyer. I had to reply to messages from my wife and from our real estate broker. This buyer was well-qualified and insisted on a specific date for a final settlement or closing on the sale in May. A quick review of my remaining plans told me that walking from Segovia was not going to work.

Command decision time. I made the decision to truncate my Camino de Madrid then and there, and to take the same train as Brigit in the morning to jump ahead to León. According to my calculations, this allowed me to change my flights home to an earlier date and make the new sale date for our home.

On the Camino, if it is not one thing it is another. What we all learn, fairly early on is that challenges and changes are inevitable and often unplanned. The experienced pilgrim assesses the challenge, thinks up alternatives for coping with the challenge, then adopts one alternative and adapts to the challenge to overcome it.

This is what I did. I had walked the first week or so of the Camino de Madrid. I would skip the remaining week or so up to León and pick up on the second half of the Camino Francés from there. I had done this half of the Camino Francés twice before, in 2013 and 2014, so it was no big deal. I knew the terrain and towns. Before going to sleep that night, I informed everyone on the other side of the pond what day I would now return home. I made the flight changes with the airline, and made advance lodging reservations for the next week or so.

When I met Brigit early the next morning, I had all my gear with me. The look on her face told me she was surprised, and not in a good way. I went up to her to explain what had happened, and that I was neither a creep, nor was I stalking her. I even showed her my e-mail traffic to confirm my change in circumstances. We rode in different classes and cars and did not see one another after that at least for several weeks. But we parted as Camino friends.

It was not until I got to León that I saw regular tranches of other pilgrims. My takeaway from this, at least in 2016 was that if you wanted a solitary pilgrimage with minimal interaction with others a springtime walk on the Camino de Madrid is for you. On the other hand, if you crave some human contact, like me, then do consider another route or another time of the year.

Some weeks later, I did see Brigit again at Santiago. She had a wonderful Camino met nice people and was very happy with the routing change. All's well that ends well.

40

This is NOT Fun Anymore
Sarria, Galicia, Spain

April 2016 (P)

The second day out of León, I left my lodgings at Hospital del Orbigo and walked towards Astorga. Having been this way twice before, I knew to expect a beautiful rural walk, through farms and small villages. But, about one-kilometer before Santibañez, the normally easy to walk cinder and gravel senda was instead slick, wet, red mud.

I had all I could do to stay vertical. There was no avoiding walking in this stuff. To both sides of the now-widened path, there was no place to walk. Even when walking in mud, on a normal Camino trail, one can usually rely on grass or weeds growing along the sides on the path to walk on to avoid getting muddy.

I struggled to stay vertical and managed to fall once onto mixed mud and gravel, hard on a hip. Finally, I straggled into Santibañez. I had a coffee at an open café while I tried to shake the caking mud from my hiking pants.

Once I continued on, the mud started again just outside the village and continued for another two kilometers or so until the terrain started up and the forest closed in. Over that distance, other pilgrims I saw were all managing to slip, slide, and fall down in the red, slimy mud. I saw an entire group of Korean pilgrims fall down like dominoes. I managed to help a couple of them to their feet before I joined them twice more on a hip, the other one, before the muddy endurance obstacle eventually ended.

To say I was angry would be an understatement. I HATE MUD! This was my fourth Camino. I had walked in rain, snow, cold, wind, and any combination of these conditions. I avoid walking in the hot dry summer season as I do not like very hot weather.

However, over all this experience, the only condition I detest is MUD. I can handle anything the Camino can throw at me. I usually find a way to adapt and overcome. But this situation was unique. There was simply no way to avoid, detour, or bypass the three kilometers of mud.

It appeared, at first, as though someone was planning to create a proper paved road. So comprehensive was the grading and leveling of the surface. It even had a slight crown, or raised center section, to allow water to run off. It was not running off, instead turning the red clay into a slimy, gooey, clingy morass.

By the time I reached David's *"Casa de los Dioses"* a few more kilometers ahead, I was simply confused. Parts of the muddy morass seemed to have a graded path on either side of the road. That year David had a lady friend, Susie if I recall correctly, living there and helping out receiving pilgrims. Fruit and beverages, and a place to stop and rest were provided for passing pilgrims.

David was not there, but Susie and I chatted and I asked her what she knew about that muddy mess several kilometers back? She told me that somehow, the local government had obtained funding to "improve" this stretch of the Camino before the next Holy Year, in 2021 – five years in the future. They set about it with determination. A contractor was hired to clear and grade, then they covered the entire graded surface with red clay as a base. The plan was for them to return to add gravel, cinders, or some other suitable soft paving topping to enable large farm equipment to pass in both directions.

How ridiculous is that? When walking these Camino routes, it is apparent that most farming is either sustenance level or small family farms. I have seen tractors, small combines, harvesters and water trucks. But I have not seen the super-sized harvesters or combines one sees on the Canadian or American plains.

My "BS" antenna started to quiver when Susie told me this last bit about widening the road for two pieces of farm equipment to easily pass. Clearly someone's brother-in-law or a friend of the family was behind this (a figure of speech). The previous senda / farm road was perfectly fine, likely for a hundred years or more. Why did they need to 'fix' it here and now?

Oh well, can't fight city hall, so to speak. I accepted it. After a nice cup of tea, I proceeded into Astorga. There I managed to find a coin laundry to properly wash my muddy outfit. You would not believe where the mud had gotten into. When I stripped off and hopped into a shower as the first order of business, the runoff was red mud for nearly ten minutes before I got the mud out of my hair, arm pits, and all the assorted nooks and crannies of my prodigious self. I had to shower and scrub off my rucksack, too.

My hiking boots were a mess. I actually soaked them in a fountain opposite the hotel to rinse them, while using a small boot brush that I carry, to get the mud out of all the seams and creases on the boots. What a mess! It took all night, stuffed with paper, to dry them on the ledge outside my window. I might have burned out the hair dryer in the hotel room, too.

I suppose I should have counted my blessings, because the next day, and for the next seven-days to Sarria it rained every day. This was not drizzle. NO, It was a steady rain, sometimes it came down in shot glasses, and sometimes in buckets. Since we all know that Santiago is not coming to us, we have to accept it and walk towards him. After all, that is what this is all about.

Earlier I mentioned that I fell on my hips twice. Now they simply hurt, and the raw weather was not helping. By the time I arrived at Molinaseca, after Cruz de Ferro, I needed a farmacia to obtain some Voltaren gel for the pain in my hips, knees and ankles. I also needed ankle support bandages.

Since I started doing the Camino in 2013, I have always had pain in both my knees. This was a follow-on effect from having been morbidly obese for about 25 years. I finally got control of the weight when I had a bariatric lap band installed in 2005. This is mentioned in the chapter on "Dirt Naps." But, the lasting effect of being so heavy was that I had to have the meniscus cartilage in both my knees trimmed when it would tear from the added weight and stress I put on them by being heavy. Losing much of the excess weight only meant the problem with my knees would not get worse. But meniscus cartilage does not regenerate. Over the years, I started having regular aches and pains. Walking the Camino just made my knees angry at me.

By 2016, my morning routine before putting my cargo pants on and booting up was to lubricate my feet with Vaseline / petroleum jelly and put two pair of socks on. Then I would rub Voltaren anti-inflammatory gel into both knees. After that, I would slide on the snug elastic knee braces I needed to provide support to my knees. Only then could I put my pants on.

This was followed by adding an 8-hour extended release, arthritis-strength pain reliever to whatever passed for breakfast. I knew from experience that my knees, and now, other bits would start to whine and complain after about an hour's walking. I preemptively medicated myself to head off the anticipated pain.

Now, we had a new dynamic. Courtesy of the slip-sliding

on the muddy road, both of my hips were now bruised and telling me they were not happy, especially in the morning. I added a good rub-down with Voltaren gel to the hips, too. Apparently, my ankles decided that they too, desired attention, so they started aching and telling me each morning that they were not amused either. Starting at Molinaseca, they got new ankle compression supports, preceded by a Voltaren massage.

This elaborate morning ritual continued for the next four days into Sarria. It continued to rain every day. That meant it rained for seven-days straight from León all the way into Sarria. By the time I walked into Sarria, my hips, knees and ankles were all rebelling in a chorus sounding a lot like "no va, no va." (I am not going. I am not going). I had booked a hotel at Sarria. I went there, checked in and did my usual daily maintenance routine.

However, everything from the waist down was hurting. My mood was very low, and I was simply not enjoying myself. There were not a lot of pilgrims about, and those I met were as grumpy as me. I had no way of knowing what physical pain they might be harboring.

I messaged my wife. Doing this, I had to consider the six-hour time difference from Spain to the eastern U.S. I recounted much of what I wrote about above. This became a two-way chat.

Finally, my wife asked, "How many of those Compostela 'thingies' do you have now anyway - well, three - so why do you need another one?" No, my wife does not do Camino. But she very kindly supports my passion for it. It took her objectivity, and being some four thousand miles away to clarify the issue.

"Take a bus into Santiago and spend time with your friends." And so, it was done. I cancelled my lodging reservations from Sarria into Santiago de Compostela, contacted my lodgings at Santiago and extended that reservation, and the next morning instead of walking up those stairs, I walked over to the bus station, took a bus to Lugo, and a connecting bus into Santiago de Compostela. Ta DA! Problem solved.

I do intend to return to Sarria one day and walk that final segment.

Got Tools?

Santiago de Compostela, Galicia, Spain

April 2016 (P/V)

My 2016 effort to walk the Camino de Madrid ended at Sarria only about 118 km or 5 days before Santiago. As already mentioned, first there was the near total absence of other pilgrims, then the urgent need to accelerate my pace to get home for an important real estate transaction, and finally, the total lack of loyalty or cooperation by my hips, knees and ankles. The rainy weather did not help either.

I arrived at Santiago five days earlier than my revised travel plans would have done, if I was able to walk from Sarria. Fortunately, I was able to modify my lodging reservations at Santiago so I could remain in place for eight days instead of the originally planned three days.

Over the years, I made a number of friends at Santiago, both at the Pilgrim Office and elsewhere around town. Reconnecting with these folks was the first thing I did after getting settled into my room. My first stop was the Pilgrim Office.

I walked over to the new Pilgrim Office, now on Rúa das Carretas. Originally, this complex was an old persons' home, where care was provided for the elderly and infirm. The campus of several large buildings had been unused for some decades before someone in charge recognized that they needed to find a much larger pilgrim office than the location on Rúa do Vilar, especially in their planning for the next coming Holy Year in 2021. From 2015 – 2016, construction progressed as funds were available. During the early months of 2016, the pilgrim office moved from Rúa do Vilar 3, to Rúa das Carretas 33.

The new campus consisted of several buildings. An architect came up with a functional plan for renovation. The results showed the thought put into this process. The main building, fronting on the street, now housed the Pilgrim Office, administrative offices, the original chapel, and an inside office for Tourism Galicia. Down the hall, there was space for large restrooms, a small Correos (post office) branch, an ALSA bus stand, a small travel agency, and more administrative offices. On the first floor there were planned multiple rooms intended as pilgrim lounges for use by different language groups, large meeting rooms, and even a proper classroom with desks. But, for 2016, only the ground floor was fully functional. The first floor was still being worked on.

An adjacent building, attached to the main building by connected hallways, was planned to contain a large pilgrim welcome lounge and waiting room on the ground floor, more offices for pilgrim related groups, and eventually, in-house dormitories for volunteer staff.

As of mid 2019, the ground floor pilgrim welcome lounge and waiting room were opened, with air conditioning, seating and smartphone charging points as well as vending machines and restrooms. Longer-term plans include installing free Wi-Fi for pilgrim use. Also, as of early 2020, the first, second and third floors were still being worked on, as funds were available.

Out back, across an open parking area for staff, was a separate utility building. It was made of several garage-type bays that had been enclosed and turned into storage areas. It is in one of these storage rooms that I found myself in mid-April 2016.

When I went to the office to say hello to my friends working there, I was in the office chatting with the senior staff when two ladies arrived. They were from the Dutch Friends of Saint James (Genootschap van Sint Jacob). This organization operates one of the most popular lounges for arriving pilgrims from that language group. We regularly received large numbers of pilgrims from the Netherlands, and they looked forward to this service on arrival at Santiago.

These ladies were there to be shown to their new, albeit temporary lounge space. The new huiskamer / lounge was eventually to be located on the first floor, upstairs from the main pilgrim office processing area. But for 2016, they were going to have to make do with one of the courtyard garage spaces.

It was here that the senior staff person took them, and asked me if I would like to see the space as well. All four of us went on a hike about 100 meters, down the stairs to the garden level, then left all the way to the end of the Pilgrim Office campus to get to the temporary space. There, the staff person gave Monica, the leader of the group, the new key and opened the room. Jill, the other Dutch lady, stood by with me.

Well, it was a space, and a rectangular one at that, but it was cold, damp and dark, the only light coming from the front windows and open door. There was perhaps one wall electrical socket in the whole space. There was no plumbing, overhead lighting, or furniture.

However, in the center of the floor was a one and a half meter tall (about six feet) stack of IKEA flatpack furniture boxes. There were perhaps 20 boxes in all. Each represented a piece of flat-pack furniture that needed to be assembled. The person from the Pilgrim Office staff gave Monica the keys to the door, left to return to work, and left us to our own devices.

Monica was a formal, well-dressed lady. She was wearing

black patent leather shoes and a medium heel, with a matching patent leather handbag on her wrist. I recall she had on white gloves. No one wore white gloves anymore, but Monica did. Her hair and makeup were perfect, her clothes were businesslike and perfect, as was her jewelry.

This is significant and relevant to the story as Jill was wearing jeans, a sweatshirt and a pair of trainers / running shoes. I was wearing my hiking clothes, now laundered.

The juxtaposition of this scene, a fancy dressed woman with handbag on arm, two more casually dressed people and a tall pile of furniture needing assembly caused the women to look at each other, and then they turned to look at me. The two ladies started laughing, really laughing. This was just after Jill had said, "Well I guess we will need to find tools and put this furniture together," Monica got a panicked look and said, "I do not know anything about tools, but I can clean."

Now, I know from having lived in the Flemish region of Belgium for two years previously that Flemish and indeed Dutch women can clean. Boy, can they ever clean! Each morning there, you can still see some older ladies literally scrubbing the sidewalk outside their homes with soap and water. We even had a saying, "There is clean, and then there is Belgian (Dutch) clean."

Anyway, I looked at them and blurted out, "Well, I arrived here five days early. This must be one of those examples of Santiago working in strange ways on the Camino. Perhaps he caused me to be here now to help." I shrugged my shoulders in the universal sign, "Why not?"

"I will help. If you ladies will fund the purchase of basic hand tools, I will help you assemble this furniture. My flight home is not for a week. I have some pieces of IKEA furniture back at home and I am familiar with it. Perhaps Jill can help, and Monica, perhaps you can do the cleaning bit?"

They agreed and we were off to the races. I opened a couple of boxes to find the instruction sheets. If you have ever assembled IKEA furniture you know they usually include pictures of the tools you need. I found and compared several of these sheets and jotted down a list of hand tools I would need. Then I left to go make the rounds of the various China Bazar shops in Santiago I knew of to assemble the tools I would need.

After about two hours or so, we all met back at the room as agreed. Monica was still "dressed to the nines" but she now sported a mop and bucket of warm sudsy water. She was going at mopping the tile floor of the new lounge space with a vengeance. This still looked more than a little absurd, but at least it was moving in the right direction.

The day was still sunny and warm, so Jill and I took one box outside and started to assemble the first of a dozen plastic scoop chairs with chrome tubular frames. That sequence went easy and took up the rest of the day. Twelve stackable scoop chairs done. We agreed to meet the next morning.

That second day, we assembled two lounge chairs and some wooden side tables. The chairs had a single, mesh seat and high-back cover over a chair-shaped tubular perimeter steel frame. The first chair easily went together in about 15 minutes.

The cover on the second chair simply would not cooperate. Jill and I tried everything we could think of to get it to slide over the tubular steel frame. We pulled and tugged, working at it for nearly two hours. Then she says, "What do the instructions say?" Ah HA! Read the directions, Dummy! What an original idea!

Well, when we both looked at the picture directions, we both noted the problem immediately, looked at each other and started laughing uncontrollably. Monica, now using a cleaning rag on the walls, was confused.

It turns out the cover was wider on the bottom of the seat / thigh-end than on the upper rear, back support area. For over two hours we have been trying to stretch the narrow end of the mesh cover over the wide end of the frame. We were putting the cover on backwards.

Less than 15 minutes later, me dripping with sweat from the effort, this chair was finished. We still talk about that to this day.

The largest piece of furniture Jill and I saved for the end so we could move the other furniture out of the way. It was a two-meter-long wooden table, resembling a picnic table, but without attached benches.

We placed the top face down on the packing carton to protect the surface, then proceeded to crawl all over each other to access various bolts and sockets, grab other components or to help each other. At times we were almost intertwined. It was comical really. Oh, to have been a fly on the (now very clean) wall.

At one point, one of the security guards happened by to get something in an adjoining storage bay, saw us crawling all over each other. He ducked his head in and just said "Get a room." Well, that did it. We disengaged, sat down and had a good laugh. It was just in time, as we needed the security guy to help us turn the table right side up anyway.

Job finished. To this day, all the Dutch volunteers use that same basket of tools. The good thing is that I know what is in the basket as I bought the tools. When I need tools for something I know exactly where to find them. Each year, as the need arises, I might add a tool or two to the collection. But everyone knows the back story.

"I Am Supposed to be Dead"
Santiago de Compostela, Galicia, Spain

April 2016 (P/V)

The morning after I finished several days of helping to assemble IKEA furniture for my Dutch friends at the new Pilgrim Office, I came out of my lodgings after having breakfast. My plan was to go see some more of my friends in and around Santiago and perhaps to do some shopping.

Over the years, I have found a number of items that I can easily buy in Spain, and in Santiago in particular, but either cannot find in the US or the items are really expensive. So as a result, it is not uncommon for me to be stopped by customs officers on the way into the US with dozens of large bars of Valor 82% dark chocolate, dozens of bars of the Heno de Previa Spanish soap I love, or multiple tubes of Voltaren anti-inflammatory cream. As of 2020, Voltaren is sold in the US.

As I exited my lodgings onto the Rúa de Acibechería, I saw a female pilgrim walking from left to right, the direction an arriving pilgrim usually comes when arriving off the Camino Francés. This woman was not in good condition. She was carrying a large rucksack with her hiking boots hanging from it. While she was using hiking poles, she was wearing cheap flip-flops and had a slight, shuffling gait. She also appeared to be in substantial pain and discomfort.

I went up to the woman right-off and asked if she spoke

English, followed by explaining that I was a volunteer at the Pilgrim Office. I asked if I could help her. She literally collapsed into my arms with tears and wracking heaving sobs and crying. I moved her to a space on the nearby rock-wall and sat her down, removed her rucksack and introduced myself by name.

She said her name was Diane and she was from the Canadian Maritime Province of Newfoundland. I asked a few basic questions. What route was she on? The Camino Francés. Where did she start? Saint Jean Pied de Port. Was she walking with anyone else? No, she was a solo walker.

I noticed that both of Diane's feet were a mess. Her blisters had blisters. She had plasters (band aids), gauze and medical tape on both her feet. I asked why she was wearing the flip-flops and not her hiking boots. She told me the boots were too small and made the blisters worse.

Then she dropped the first of several bombshell pronouncements on me. Sobbing, she explained that she was a stage four breast cancer survivor. She was supposed to be dead, not walking a Camino. When she was told she was in remission, and the chemotherapy treatment ended, she vowed to make this pilgrimage to give thanks and to prove she could overcome anything life might throw at her.

I asked where she was headed when I found her. She said she was going to the Pilgrim Office to get her Compostela. I explained that I happened to be going that way to see my friends there. I explained that I arrived early off my Camino from Madrid and was helping out around the office, and that I would be pleased to help her finish her Camino.

Then, Diane told me that she had a very depleted immune system and was very afraid of getting infections from her blistered feet. I suggested that we first work to get her to the office, then figure out how best to get her some appropriate care for her feet.

I put on her rucksack and gave her the walking sticks. We proceeded very slowly down the street, through the arch under the Archbishop's residence, to Praza Obradoiro. There, in front of the Parador, I congratulated her on officially finishing her Camino and pointed out the bronze marker in the center of the plaza that marked the official distance zero to the Cathedral. We continued down the ramp to Rúa das Carretas towards the Pilgrim office.

As we were shuffling along, Diane told me that her best friend, with whom she had endured several years of chemo and radiation treatments for breast cancer, had died two days earlier. The funeral would be tomorrow. Recounting this made her cry all the harder and deeper. She had to lean on me several times.

Diane was all the more upset because there was no way she could be back to Canada to say good bye to her friend with whom she had shared one of the most horrible of life's journeys. Evidently, the friend knew she had no treatment options left when she encouraged Diane to go do the Camino for both of them. The friend followed Diane's progress every day even as her health declined.

When we got to the office, I escorted Diane past the security guards at the front door and took her into the chapel. The chapel is original to the building when it was a care facility for elderly and infirm residents, run by the church. The altar piece or retablo is incredibly beautiful, as are various statues, stained glass and original wooden furnishings. Everything was renovated to like-new condition when the office was repurposed as the new Pilgrim Office.

I ushered Diane to a pew to sit with her rucksack and sticks nearby. Having helped other pilgrims with emotional burdens to unload, I sort of knew what might happen. I had a package of facial tissues in my cargo pocket so I gave it to Diane. I told her I needed to go into the office to arrange to take her directly in without standing on the long line. She clearly did not have strength left for that.

She looked at me to say thank you and I suggested she reflect on Him – pointing to the altar and the ornate carved retablo behind it, as well as the statue of the Virgin Mary. I explained briefly that the chapel is dedicated to Our Lady of the Cures (*Nuestra Señora de los Remedios*).

Diane looked at me with big eyes and said aloud, but I am not a Catholic. I replied, "I don't care, and neither does He! Just ask in silence. Express your feelings. I do not care what your religious tradition is. This is a place of healing. Allow yourself to be healed. I'll be back shortly." More hugs, a LOT more tears.

I went into the office and explained the situation to the staff that I knew well, and regarded almost as a second family. Of course, I could bring Diane in the back way directly into the administrative office where one of the women on staff with better English skills would happily help.

I returned to Diane in the chapel. She was taking me up on my offer to let it all out. She had gone through the packet of tissues and there was mascara everywhere. I picked up her gear and we passed through a back way directly into the administrative offices. This was done occasionally with pilgrims who could not wait in the single queue. Unwritten policy and common sense called for them to be accommodated as inconspicuously and quickly as possible.

We got Diane seated in front of an office desk. I brought her water to drink. The staff person examined her credencial. I explained to Diane that, having walked all the way from Saint Jean Pied de Port she could choose to have the optional Distance Certificate to commemorate this achievement. Yes, thank you, she wanted that.

Then, I explained to the staff person about the best friend who had just passed away and pointed out to Diane that Catholic Church teaching is that a person obtaining a Compostela could dedicate that accomplishment to the soul of a deceased or very ill person, typically a family member or very close friend, who would never be able to make a Camino on their own. This meant she could have the name of her recently deceased friend added to the document "in vicare pro." I explained this was Latin for "in place of."

Diane exclaimed "Oh God, you're not serious?" "Yes, I am very serious." The staff person chimed in saying this was not a problem, they do it every day, and all she needed was the full name of the person she wanted to dedicate this to. More, deep, wracking sobs, shaking and tears.

Diane went on to explain through her crying, that her friend was Catholic and this would mean so much to her surviving family. I asked the staff person for a duplicate Compostela so Diane could present one to the friends' family and have one for herself. I also asked for the requisite Certificate of Distance.

Absenting myself briefly, I went to buy a tubo (cardboard tube) and to pay for the Certificate of Distance for Diane. It seemed improper to ask her to pay for anything. With the tubo and receipt I returned to the office. We presented the certificates to Diane, rolled them into the tubo and returned the tubo and her credencial – all stamped and official.

The next step was what to do about her feet. Diane decided that, if she could get to a decent hotel, find a farmacia, and get the necessary supplies, she could dress her feet. I hopped onto the internet and used my Booking.com account to find a business-class hotel. Asking Diane what her budget was, I located a four-star business hotel about a kilometer away in the area known as the "Ensanche" – the newer flat area of town, on Avenida de Rosalia de Castro. In years past, I had learned, and as I explained, staying at this level of hotel guaranteed English-speaking front desk staff. Diane agreed and I made the reservation.

She then asked how we were going to get there. I turned to the staff person who had so wonderfully helped Diane through this entire thing. All I said was we need a taxi to go to this address (the hotel) as soon as possible, and that I would escort her there to make sure she was okay. The phone was picked up and a call was made.

We no sooner got outside in front than a taxi appeared. Rúa das Carretas is a pedestrianized street, but local residents, taxis and emergency vehicles are permitted to drive on the one-way concourse. In ten minutes, we were at the hotel. I helped Diane into the lobby. We explained to the desk clerk that I had made the reservation but it was for Diane and she was paying for it.

Once we got that sorted, I explained to the desk staff that Diane had a chronic illness and was susceptible to infections. Her feet were a mess and she needed a really good farmacia.

The hotel staff was wonderful. They told Diane that once she got settled in, to provide them a list, in English, of whatever she needed and they would send someone to the farmacia down the street to obtain whatever she needed. They even included the possibility of antibiotics or stronger pain medication, especially if Diane had her Canadian prescription labels or a doctor's note. She did.

As all of this sank in Diane lost it one more time. She could simply not believe that everyone was being so nice, helpful and kind to her.

My answer to Diane was to explain, that is our purpose. We are all one big Camino family. We look out for and help one another, and we never leave anyone behind.

The last time I saw Diane was when the elevator doors closed as she went up to her room. We hugged, more tears, she thanked me. I told her she was most welcome and it was our privilege to be of some assistance. I wished her "Buen Camino" and walked back into the old town and to my original planned activities for that day.

To this day, I wonder and pray that Diane is healthy and living a good life with her loved ones.

Nicole, My Friend

Santiago de Compostela, Galicia, Spain

July 2016 (V)

By the third year of my volunteering at the Pilgrim Office in Santiago de Compostela, I developed a preference for being in Santiago during the busiest time of the entire pilgrimage year. This is generally during the months of July and August. Because my wife would only allow me to be away from home for about a month, and to be of as much help as possible during the busiest time at the Pilgrim Office, I started to volunteer from mid-July through mid-August each summer.

The busiest time for pilgrim arrivals at the Pilgrim Office was the week before and after the annual Feast of Santiago on 25 July, and then for the Catholic Feast of the Assumption of the Blessed Virgin Mary on 15 August. For some reason, huge numbers of Spanish and Portuguese pilgrims swelled the daily arrivals at the Pilgrim Office to several thousand daily. It did not matter how many volunteers there were. There were always a huge number of pilgrims to welcome and process.

Such was the case when I arrived at the Pilgrim Office on a Monday morning in July 2016 to start four weeks of volunteer work. There I was greeted by other volunteers who had started days or weeks earlier and with whom I would work.

One of the volunteers, already there to greet me, was a young woman from New Brunswick, Canada, via her then current home in Glasgow, Scotland. Nicole Bourque ('bork') would become one of the best friends that I ever made on Camino or while volunteering. She was funny, very funny in fact, brilliant - no beyond brilliant - and just a pleasure to be around.

We first met at the Pilgrim Office that Monday morning. A staff person told us the address of our flat, and gave us keys to the building and the actual apartment flat. The newly arriving volunteers were told to go to the flat, unpack and return to the office to go for a Cathedral tour laid on for 16:00. Off we went.

This was the same flat, perched above the train station, that I had stayed in the previous year, and which I already wrote briefly about here. However, this year, I scored the room with the large bed, yippee! On the other hand, from the windows, I could read the destination boards on some of the train tracks at the train station, with a pair of binoculars. Yup! We were literally on top of that damned train station – again! At least I knew exactly what to expect. I started to make a mental shopping list. Ear plugs went on the top of that list.

I went to the flat, unpacked in my large room facing the train station, listened to some train announcements, and felt right at home. Next, I headed out to the supermarket, a couple of blocks up the adjacent Rúa do Hórreo to obtain supplies, and to locate earplugs.

Later, when I returned to the Pilgrim Office as requested, Nicole was just finishing a shift at 15:00. I had on my "Voluntario" t-shirt that we all wore to alert the pilgrims that we worked at the office. The group assembled and we proceeded, including Nicole, to the Cathedral.

There, that day, we would tour the archeological site underneath the Cathedral, the literal foundation of the cathedral, dating back to the first century AD. It was great that Nicole was there because she spoke fluent Spanish and translated.

These tours are always and only offered in Spanish. On the other hand, the person conducting the tour is usually the top lay or clerical person on the Cathedral staff and THE subject matter expert. If you asked a question, and assuming you could understand the reply, you got directly the best possible information available anywhere. Well, I had lots, no tons of questions, and Nicole handled the translation like a champ.

Our tour guide was the Catholic priest who was also a university lecturer in history and the official historian of the Cathedral and its archives. He had forgotten more about the history of everything related to the Cathedral and the entire cult of the Camino than most scholars ever knew.

After the tour, we were released for the day and told to report for work the following morning at 10:00 am. Nicole and I agreed to have tapas and drinks on our way back to the flat. She was already housed there in one of the four rooms.

Along the way, Nicole said we should stop at a particular place "O Recuncho d'Fonso" for drinks as it was her favorite place. It was directly on Rúa do Hórreo, it was on the way to the flat, and was downhill. I thought great! If I have a little too much to drink, at least it will not be far.

We sat at a table outside on the sidewalk. Nicole introduced me to the proprietor, Alfonso. They had an excellent pan-European beer list. Even some of my favorite Belgian beers from my time living there were offered. Drinks were ordered and the generous tapas followed.

Nicole told me this story. A couple of years before, she was in Santiago after one of her Caminos. A friend, back in Glasgow, Scotland, was minding her pet fish, Santiago. Nicole was a senior lecturer in cultural anthropology at Glasgow University.

Anyway, one day, she receives a phone call from her friend Robert who was minding Santiago while she was away. He was bereft with grief. Nicole's beloved pet goldfish Santiago had passed away. Robert found him floating in his little bowl one morning.

Well, Nicole was very, very upset. Finishing her work at the Pilgrim Office, and though very upset, she managed to walk down the street towards the volunteer flat. Along the way, she happens on O Recuncho d'Fonso and stops in for a drink and some tapas, but mostly for a drink.

Sitting at the bar, Alfonso comes to serve her. At this time, she does not know Alfonso as she had never before been in this bar and restaurant. She orders a beer and, as is the case the world over, the bartender is the next best thing to a priest in the confessional. Nicole tearfully, very tearfully, tells Alfonso about how her best friend has died unexpectedly. They are both speaking in Spanish. She goes on praising Santiago for his intelligence and loving spirit.

Now, Alfonso, being a Spaniard is possessed of "duende." Duende is a chivalrous spirit that most Spanish men seem to be born with. It does not quite translate that way, instead being defined literally as an imp or an elf. But, in the Spanish culture, a man simply cannot allow a woman to be in distress or to be upset without diving in to try to help in some way, in any way within his means. It is virtually a cultural imperative. Seeing a crying woman causes this spirit of chivalry or duende to well up. It demands to be satisfied.

Alfonso pours Nicole a generous measure of scotch whiskey, as Nicole had mentioned she lived in Glasgow, Scotland. Hence, all Scots must like Scotch whiskey. Little does he know that Nicole does, indeed, like her Scotch whiskey.

She is blathering on and on though her wracked sobs about poor, poor Santiago and how miserable she is to be here and not there, when he needs her. The first glass of scotch goes down, to be replaced by a second, then a third… por supuesto (of course)! Duende demands it. Alfonso being, well, an honorable Spanish man, does not charge her for these drinks. He is doing his duty.

As this sobbing, now alcohol-reinforced conversation goes back and forth, Nicole is going on about her "pescito" (pes-kee-toh) Santiago, and happens to mention that Santiago was just a poor tiny fish in a bowl, but to her, he was a giant… Alfonso is REALLY confused now. What! A fish? This woman is upset over a dead fish?

You had to be there, hearing Nicole relate this story more than a year afterwards. By now, she is shaking with laughter and quivering like a really large Jello-mold dessert. Nicole is not a petite woman, but the laugher is coming from her toes, she is literally crying by now. The tears of laughter are rolling down her cheeks as she tried to convey Alfonso's reaction to finding out that Santiago is her gold fish and not a human.

As she relates this story, this simply does not register with Alfonso. When a Galician is presented with a dead fish, the automatic questions include: do you want it prepared baked, boiled, broiled or grilled? Followed closely by, do you want sauce with that? Alfonso is stunned, then Nicole goes on about her pesca. Little fish…

The original conversation ended with Nicole apologizing for being so emotional over the loss of a pet fish. She even offered to pay for all the scotch. But, Alfonso, he was just trying to console a distraught Nicole over the loss of her giant of a friend Santiago, out of a sense of duende. Well, the free scotch stopped.

When we returned to the Pilgrim Office to work the next day, Nicole related an abbreviated version of this story to one of the other volunteers, Pepe, who came up from Sevilla. Pepe was very confused too, even though he knew that Santiago was a pet fish. He politely corrected Nicole's use of the word 'pescado' meaning fish or 'pescito' meaning something like 'little fish.'

Pepe explained that the correct term for a pet fish was "pez" with the 'z' pronounced like 'th' or "peth." Now, Nicole laughed all the more as she recounted the year-old story of meeting Alfonso and all that free scotch. It was, and is still a very funny story. Later that month, we were to locate a café in the Ensanche, the newer, flat section of Santiago, named El Pez, the pet fish. Well, go figure!

Over the next several weeks, Nicole and I had several other very funny experiences. But I want to take the liberty, as the author, I can take liberties to tell you about my good friend Nicole. I only knew her for four months.

After our few weeks together at Santiago she returned to Scotland and I to the US. In October, we again met at the annual Symposium on Pilgrimage organized by the Pilgrimage Studies Department at the College of William and Mary in Williamsburg, Virginia. Nicole presented an academic paper on the pilgrimage rites of certain tribes in Ecuador. It was fascinating. Her interest in and devotion to all things pilgrimage-related was near global, like her personality.

Then about three weeks later, I received a phone call from my good friend Johnnie Walker at Santiago to relate this about my friend Nicole Bourque:

Dr. Lisa Nicole Bourque
1966–2016
"It is with heavy hearts and great sadness that the family of Dr. Nicole Bourque, announce her sudden and unexpected passing at her home in Glasgow, Scotland.
"Nicole was born in Fredericton, New Brunswick, July 25th, 1966. She graduated from Fredericton High School in 1984 and went to the University of New Brunswick,

where she completed a degree in Anthropology with First Class Honors. Her outstanding scholarship earned her a prestigious Commonwealth Scholarship, which funded her pursuit of a PhD at the University of Cambridge (Girton College). Nicole won an O'Brian Foundation award to fund her fieldwork in Ecuador, which resulted in her outstanding thesis "Of Soups, Saints and Sucres."

"Nicole received her PhD in 1993 and joined the faculty in the School of Social and Political Sciences at the University of Glasgow, where she spent her whole career, her final position being that of Senior Lecturer in Social Anthropology.

"Nicole was deeply committed to her work, her students, and her faculty colleagues. An open, friendly and caring person with a winning personality (and a good listener), her expansive knowledge and easy manner made her a stellar conversationalist. She was bubbling with life and made so many long-lasting friendships everywhere she went.

"Apart from her life as a scholar, Nicole was a free spirit who, the moment her work was done, loved to travel. Over the years she visited dozens of countries and became somewhat of a polyglot.

"Nicole was a mountain climbing enthusiast and climbed mountains all over the world. She was only the second Canadian woman to climb all 282 Munros in Scotland and the first from New Brunswick to do so. Munros are mountains that are over 3000 feet in height (914 meters).

"Nicole was very humble despite her many accomplishments, too numerous to mention here. Her passing leaves a big void at the University of Glasgow, and among her colleagues, students, friends, and family."

That last statement in Nicole's obituary was the biggest understatement I have ever experienced. Simply put, "she was a very good friend, albeit for far too-brief a time, and is missed to this day." Here is Nicole with another volunteer at the Pilgrim Office.

44

Miss Hot Pants!

Santiago de Compostela, Galicia, Spain

July 2016 (V)

The volunteers at the Pilgrim Office were housed at one of three apartment flats the Pilgrim Office rented around the new part of Santiago de Compostela. As I mentioned, I got lucky and drew the large student flat that overlooked the train station. I say lucky for two reasons. It was closest to the Pilgrim Office, with most of the shops one might need on the way, and the rather loud public announcements of trains arriving and departing only lasted until midnight. The other two flats for volunteers were in a building directly upstairs and across the street from a couple of all-night bars that attracted large numbers of young and very noisy people partying until dawn each day. It was worst on Friday and Saturday nights.

For 2016, I was blessed in several ways. One was my association with Nicole. Another arrived one morning, early in my month-long volunteer stint. His name was Berndt, from the French Alps, east of the French city of León. Berndt had walked a long Camino to arrive at Santiago and volunteered to help. We had a couple of empty rooms, so the deal was done.

Berndt was a proper older gentleman and so friendly. One of the generous things he would do is to go to a fresh fruit market up the street each day and prepare individual, fresh fruit salads for each of us in the flat – every morning. Not only were the salads large, but clearly, Berndt knew how to cook.

One afternoon at the Pilgrim Office, Father Juan, one of the priests we knew from the Cathedral staff, came to speak to the office managers and then to Nicole. I mentioned she spoke fluent Spanish. Juan, the priest, did not speak any English. All Nicole would tell me is that we were going to have a fourth roommate this evening.

We finished our shifts and went home. I recall we prepared a meal that night. The three of us, Nicole, Berndt and me. I was right when I mentioned earlier that Berndt could cook. Wow! The meal was simple, with small but very well prepared and presented courses. Plus, he had selected a nice Albariño, a local white wine, to accompany the meal.

As we were cleaning up and just hanging out, the doorbell rang. Nicole answered the door. Standing there was Father Juan from the office, together with a very pretty young girl carrying a largish rucksack. Nicole invited them in, and we learned that Lisa was Father Juan's niece. His brother was Lisa's dad. She was 20, if I recall correctly.

But, did I say she was pretty? No that is an understatement. She might have been a model. Lisa was that pretty. She was wearing a t-shirt and cut-off denim jeans that, in the US we would call Daisy Duke's, after a female character in a 1980's US television show. Let's just say these shorts were cut so high that her gluteus maximus was showing. I doubt Father Juan ever noticed, as he did not walk behind her. But the three of us certainly noticed.

The gist of the entire deal was that Lisa's parents wanted her away from their hometown for the summer. She worked as a teacher's assistant and was off for the summer months as schools were closed. I could understand this parental concern, as I could sense the waves of young female hormones just flooding from this pretty young lady.

Father Juan organized a volunteer assignment at the office for his niece. It turns out that in addition to Spanish Lisa spoke very good English and French. This combination of languages made her very useful indeed. After she worked for two weeks, Lisa was planning to do a Camino.

After we shared a glass of wine, Father Juan explained to Nicole that he wanted Lisa to stay with us, in our flat because we were good Catholic adults and would look after her. Did I note a subtext here?

After perhaps 15 minutes, Father Juan departed and we were all in the living room. Berndt went to the kitchen to finish cleaning up from dinner. I looked at Nicole and she looked at me. We exchanged a knowing look. I said to Nicole, "Do you want to play the bad parent or the good parent? It seems that Juan made us foster parents."

We asked Lisa to come back into the living room for a moment once she got her gear unpacked in the extra bedroom. As she returned, Nicole started by saying that Father Juan left us responsible for you. We know you are an adult, but since we are all living together sharing this flat, there are a few ground rules. Tom will explain those rules." Gee, thanks a lot, she made me the heavy. Okay, here goes.

"Lisa, first let us say that we are happy to have you here. You will be a big help in the office and your language skills are very good. But, as your uncle made us sort of temporary parents, we feel the need to establish some rules. We know that, under the law you are considered an adult. But, believe it or not, we have all been your age at one time. We understand more than we look like we do. Plus, as we have all come to learn over the years, that in the Church, the rules are somewhat fluid. We need to adapt so that everyone is happy.

"Rule Number One, (as I walk to the front door and open it) do you see that threshold at the bottom of the door? That is a line. We know that you are a very attractive young woman, and we believe you have to beat off the young men with a stick back home, but here, here is the rule.

"When you are on the outside of that line, you are responsible for your behavior, the friends you make, and what you do or do not do. However, on this side, the inside of that line, we three are responsible for what happens to you here. No one is permitted in this flat unless they are a volunteer in the office or your uncle – no friends – no way! We do not want to have to explain anything to your uncle. God forbid!

"Rule Number Two, we pick up after ourselves. Mama Nicole and papas Tom and Berndt do not pick up your stuff, nor do we do your laundry. We expect you to keep your room neat. We will show you where everything is.

"Rule Number Three, we share and we help each other, but we do not keep score. If you take something from the refrigerator or cabinet, just let us know so we can replace it. What is ours is yours, and we are happy to share.

"Got it? Okay, Fine. Now let's have fun."

For the remainder of that two-week period, we all had a very enjoyable time. Lisa was like having a daughter. The funny thing is that neither Nicole, Berndt, nor I had children of our own. This was a new experience. We opted to try to behave more like older siblings than authoritarian parents. To be fair, Lisa was a very mature and well-behaved young woman. Everything went well.

At the end of this two-week period, Nicole departed to return to Glasgow, Scotland. Berndt left to do another Camino, then return to his home in France. I was staying for another two weeks so new roommates would arrive. As the end of the two weeks approached, we also had the chore to get Lisa ready for her Camino. She decided that she would take the bus from Santiago to O'Cebreiro, and walk back to Santiago from there. This would nominally be about 10 days.

The backpack she had with her was too large, at about 70 liters; so, I put out a call around the office for someone to loan us a smaller rucksack. After a few days, someone brought a 40-liter bag from home. This was closer to what Lisa would need, but the problem was that Lisa had a short torso and the rucksack was for a taller person.

I solved this problem by obtaining four kitchen sponges, two microfiber dish towels and some duck-tape. Remember, you can do anything with duck-tape. Taking two sponges, I used one dish cloth to 'giftwrap' the pair of sponges and used duck-tape to secure this package. With my supplies, I constructed two such shoulder pads. To hold them in place, I used four heavy-duty rubber bands, two to a side. This contraption closed all the air space between the rucksack shoulder straps and Lisa's shoulders. This allowed us to properly adjust the rucksack for her shorter torso.

One evening, we laid out all the things Lisa thought she was going to take on Camino so I could help her refine her packing. Some exchanges and deletions were made. I told her that she could leave behind everything she was not taking, here in the flat. As I would still be here when she returned, getting these items would not be a problem. Together, we managed to get her pack weight down.

One thing I could not get her to do was to not wear cotton underwear. On the Camino, as a general rule, cotton is to be avoided. It holds moisture, does not dry fast enough, and increases friction on skin. But Lisa was intent on wearing her very brief, lady briefs.

The night before she was to leave by bus, I went to the local supermercado and bought her a gift that I knew she would come to rely on. It was a shallow tub or round tin of Nivea moisturizing skin cream. When I gave it to her, Lisa was very confused. I told her to just trust me, the day will come on Camino when she would kill for this. Okay, into the rucksack it went.

Lisa departed the next morning to the bus station to get her bus back east to O'Cebreiro. I went back to work at the Pilgrim Office. We had exchanged cellphone numbers so she could text, or reach out if she had any problems.

For the next couple of days, things were silent. Then one morning, I check my text messages. There was one from Lisa that simply said, in Spanish… "soy irritado" (I am irritated). I knew exactly what she was referring to. I texted her back… (1) Use the Nivea where the irritation is; and (2) at the next town try to buy a couple pair of synthetic fabric underwear… All she said was "Thank you."

A week later she showed up at the Pilgrim Office to get her Compostela. She thanked me for being smarter than her and said she should have listened. I explained that in my long history with women, I have learned never to try to change them. The gift of the Nivea cream was my way of getting you prepared for what I knew would happen. Sometimes the trick is to help someone without letting them know they are being helped.

Lisa came back to the flat for a couple of days as we had a temporarily available room. She then departed for her home.

After this small, defined experience with being responsible for a young person, I no longer wonder about not having children of my own. The parents can have it.

45

Holy Smoke!

Santiago de Compostela, Galicia, Spain

August 2016 (V)

Each summer, about every two weeks, Pilgrim Office volunteers are presented certificates thanking them for their volunteer service. These presentations are generally made in the Cathedral, after a Pilgrim Mass.

To facilitate this, the volunteers are asked to sit inside the ornate, wooden altar railing. Normally, only VIPs and visiting dignitaries from Spain or around the world sit inside the rail. For example, when the King or Queen of Spain are present, they sit inside the rail. Of course, they get a high-backed comfortable chair to sit in. We volunteers sit on the hard, wooden benches.

The Pilgrim Mass is quite impressive, especially when it concludes with the Botafumeiro ceremony. In the beginning, and stories conflict on this, the Botafumeiro was used: (1) to collect all the prayers of the faithful and offer them in a sweet smoke to God; or (2) bestow God's blessings on the assembled faithful; or to (3) to overcome the intense odor of the really dirty and smelly pilgrims who filled the Cathedral, at least hundreds of years ago.

Traditionally a censer, also called an incenser, a much smaller version of the humongous Botafumeiro, is used in Catholic Masses and other ceremonies such as weddings or funerals to bless the bride and groom, or the casket / coffin of the deceased person. At various times during the Catholic liturgical year, a smaller incenser is used to bless the altar or the assembled congregation by swinging the lit and smoking censer to spread the aromatic incense inside, all about.

Whether one is using a small incenser or a Botafumeiro, also called by some of my Australian friends a barbie (barbeque) on a rope… it is filled with aromatic incense, which is lit to produce a fragrant scent. The scent can vary.

Having served as a volunteer at the Pilgrim Office for seven years, I have had the privilege to be included in the groups of volunteers to be thanked in this manner many times. Usually, we are told to appear in our volunteer t-shirts. The ushers and security folks escort us inside the wooden altar rail, and we sit on the benches for the entire Mass, certificate presentation, and Botafumeiro ceremony.

In August 2016, when I was included in the group of volunteers to receive thank you certificates, I happened to end up sitting on the very end of a very full wooden bench on the north side of the altar. This was very near where the eight red-robed tiraboleiros, the men who pull the heavy ropes to maneuver the Botafumeiro through the swinging arc, typically stand.

After the Communion portion of the Mass, and before the final blessing and the Botafumeiro ceremony, we were presented our certificates by the Archbishop and the Dean of the Cathedral. After the presentation, we returned to our seats. A group photo would be taken after the entire ceremony was concluded.

I mentioned I was seated on the very end of the wooden bench. One of the tiraboleiros opened a portion of the altar rail right next to me. This was, as I was to find out, to allow the Botafumeiro to swing through its full arc, but less than one meter off the ground. In previous years I had never paid particular attention to this small detail. But now I was intrigued.

The presiding priest pronounces the final blessing, and the formal Mass is concluded. Now the organ starts up for the traditional hymn to Santiago, and the tiraboleiros get ready to do their thing. The lead tiraboleiro ignites the incense inside the Botafumeiro, and the other tiraboleiros start to heave on the thick heavy rope.

As they pull up and down on the rope, the lit Botafumeiro starts to rise and fall. Then, one of the tiraboleiros gives it a mighty shove to start it swinging in an arc. I do not profess to fully understand the rope and pulley system that has been used for many hundreds of years to make this all work. However, it is truly ingenious.

A combination of the pulling action, plus the starting of the arc by the great shove, results in the awesome sight of this solid silver "barbie on a rope" swinging at over 70 kilometers per hour, nearly a hundred meters, in an arc that goes from the north transept of the Cathedral to the south transept.

If you have not seen this in person at least once in your life, you should. It really is incredible. If you cannot do so, then go to You Tube and query "Botafumeiro, Santiago de Compostela." Hundreds of pilgrims and tourists have video recorded this ceremony and it is easily viewable.

As the Botafumeiro is picking up speed and extending the arc outwards, each time it passes by I can SEE the fire inside the silver container. I can FEEL the heat from the incense on fire as it passes on each arc. I can SMELL the incense as it washes over me.

As a Cradle Catholic the smell brings back many memories from my life. It is not unpleasant, just very profound. The Botafumeiro, or "barbie on a rope," is passing perhaps six inches or fifteen centimeters from my left arm.

I had a momentary burst of emotion. I leaned to the volunteer sitting next to me and commented, "I now understand the full meaning of the colloquial saying Holy Smoke!" This experience literally immersed me in that phrase. It is an experience I shall always treasure… a real AH HA moment!

46

Living Under the Bridge
Ponte de Lima, Portugal

May 2017 (P)

In May 2017, while walking the latter half of the Camino Portuguese, from Lisbon to Santiago de Compostela, I was passing through Ponte de Lima, where I had a reserved hotel room. After checking in, I joined a group of pilgrims from assorted countries at an outdoor café for a few pre-dinner beers. Introductions were made, and we began to learn of each other's backgrounds.

It was then that I met my first-ever "Camino Hobo" or "Hobogrini." This is my term for someone who has disconnected from their previous life and lives exclusively on the Camino. They frequently have no permanent home. How they earn, find or obtain money to exist on is, frankly, a puzzle to me.

In the years and Caminos since, I have encountered more of these folks. Some appear to have emotional or substance abuse issues, others might have been disowned by families, and others may just have "gone native" as we sometimes say. This latter group sometimes actually believes that they are pilgrims of days gone by.

In concept, this is similar to a formal diagnosed condition in Jerusalem, called "The Jerusalem Syndrome." In Israel, psychiatrists see several hundred cases of people from all over the world who delve into the first century biblical world, then somehow, get lost and descend further into this delusion.

I am not a medical professional, but I can say that sometimes these folks are gentle souls who would not harm a fly. Others seem to be more malevolent.

On this occasion, while sitting around the table enjoying our Portuguese Super Bock beer, we were joined by a bearded, long-haired fellow named Silvester. He claimed to be the "white sheep" of his Polish family. Silvester explained that all of his family were petty criminals, drunks, and addicts. But he was different. He had gotten away from this dysfunctional family, and was proud to say he had been living on the various Camino routes for 15 years.

He was dressed appropriately, but his canvas shoes appeared to be held together with duck-tape, and they were too light duty for serious Camino walking. That was a curious detail.

Silvester's English was quite good and as he hand-rolled the first of many cigarettes, others asked him questions about life on the road. Where did he sleep? He usually checked into the nearest donativo albergue, but only to use the facilities, bathe and wash his clothes. But he made a fine point of saying he preferred to sleep out of doors. He had a lightweight, pop-up tent and explained that he usually waited until it was nearly sunset, then pitched his tent, usually under the nearest bridge.

Silvester explained that he preferred living under a bridge, as being in a closed room with others gave him bad dreams. Plus, he did like to drink. He said that after having something to eat, his custom was to buy a bottle of inexpensive wine and drink himself to sleep under the bridge.

Then someone asked how he made money to live on. Silvester explained that he actually needed only maybe five Euros daily to survive. For clothing, he relied on donativo boxes at donativo albergues. He had a busking or street entertainment scheme involving breathing fire and juggling with lit batons. He would place the fiery batons in his mouth to ignite the flames, then close his mouth to extinguish the flames.

He went on to explain that he knew the formula to make this work, and he could easily obtain all the ingredients in any farmacia. He would mix his concoction, pick a spot, then juggle fiery batons and make fire come out of his mouth. People tossed coins into his hat on the street in front of him. I had seen this sort of amusement elsewhere in Europe. As a result, it seemed to make sense to me.

I asked Silvester how he managed the winters. He explained that in November, as traffic on the most popular northern Camino routes waned, he tended to remain in the south of Spain where the temperature was milder and there were a lot of seasonal and religious festivals where he could earn money. He knew which albergues stayed open all year and which were donativo. When he was able, he said he donated something, even just a couple of Euros.

After our drinks, the table of assorted pilgrims split up to go their own ways for the rest of the evening.

The next morning, walking out of Ponte de Lima, I met Jacques, a Belgian man who had been at the table the evening before. He was wearing sports sandals with socks, and swearing a lot, in English, French and Flemish – which I understood. He had stayed at the same donativo albergue mentioned by Silvester, but had slept there, and not under the bridge like our friendly fire-breathing pilgrim.

But, when everyone claimed their hiking shoes and boots from the front hallway of the albergue, his were missing. After searching all over, he concluded that someone unknown had taken them in the night. The good news was that he had another pair of footwear to hold him over until he could get to the next town with a proper shoe store where he might replace his boots.

However, Jacques was infuriated because he had worn those boots for years while he was a police officer in Belgium, before he retired two years earlier. The boots had been regularly resoled and fit him like a glove. I understood his situation as my hiking boots had been re-soled twice already, and they had been broken in perfectly for my feet.

As we walked along, I wondered aloud if he had noticed the poor condition of Silvester's footwear the previous evening. He said he did not, so I filled him in. I asked him if he noticed a pair of decrepit shoes such as this in any trash bin in or near the albergue. He said he did not, then got very angry.

Jacques's said that, if Silvester needed money for shoes, why did he not just ask the group of us at the table. I agreed that we might have contributed for him to buy a pair of boots, as Ponte de Lima had several shops where hiking boots could be had. Jacques was angrier that his best and favorite pair of boots had been stolen. He felt like a part of him was taken, like an arm or leg.

On the Camino, money comes and money goes. It is lost and it is found. But a good-fitting, comfortable pair of hiking shoes or boots, ah, that is something worth its weight in gold.

We never did nail this down, nor are we ever likely to know.

Living in a Convent
Santiago de Compostela, Galicia, Spain

July 2017 (V)

After the 2016 pilgrim season, many local property owners in Santiago de Compostela took their previously student-rented flats off the student and open rental market to convert them into Air BnB flats. This created an immediate ripple affect across the city increasing costs for student housing and for housing for Pilgrim Office volunteers during the summer months. In the case of the Pilgrim Office volunteer flats, the owners doubled the monthly rental fee, placing these flats out of the reach of the Cathedral and Pilgrim Office.

In reply, officials on the Cathedral staff searched about for a solution. A most original solution was found over the winter of 2016–2017, before the 2017 pilgrim and volunteer season would start. Connections were made, phone calls occurred, and a deal was done.

On the Avenida de San Roque, up the hill from the Cathedral, there sits a massive stone building that occupies the full block from one street to another. It is several hundred meters long and looks like a castle.

This massive edifice is the Convento do Santa Clara de Asís (the Convent of Saint Clare of Assisi). This enclosed, cloistered convent of the Order of St. Clare was founded in 1260 with private donations and the dowry of Doña Violante of Castile, wife of King Alfonso X the Wise. Dating from the 13th century, the original buildings were enlarged in the 16th century with donations from Doña Isabel of Granada, the abbess of the convent.

Most of what can be seen today was built between the 17th and 18th centuries. Made from granite, the convent is arranged in three sections. There is a cloister and within it a church. It is a curtain front that gives way to a small garden where the true and simple facade of the church is hidden. The main building once housed several hundred "Clarisas" as the sisters were called.

Today, only seven Clarisas still live in the convent. In addition to their regular daily prayers, they do things for the Cathedral, like embroidery, laundry or ironing. In fact, the nun who has been singing the ritual *Hymn to Santiago* at each Botafumeiro ceremony at the Cathedral is one of the remaining Clarisas.

The third component of this campus is the building at the southwest corner providing the main entry to the cloister and church as well as to the main convent where the cloistered sisters still live today. Above the entry vestibule and gates is the Vicaría or vicarage. As the name implies, this is where the several priests who were assigned to attend to the spiritual needs of the cloistered Clarisas lived.

It is here that the deal was made to house Pilgrim Office volunteers beginning with the 2017 pilgrim season. It was here I was taken in mid-July 2017 when I arrived at the Pilgrim Office to take up my annual monthly volunteer assignment. I say taken because one look at the hill that one had to ascend, to travel from the Pilgrim Office to the convent was enough for me to tell the staff to find a car or call a taxi. I was not lugging my luggage up that hill.

A car was found to take the luggage and we met at the

Vicarage. This building was HUGE. Everything was out-sized. The outer doors were like huge castle gates. The door from the entry vestibule to the Vicarage proper was about three meters tall and a meter and a half wide. On the inside was a massive iron bar intended to lock the closed door by connecting the center of the very thick solid wood door to the meter-thick granite blocks.

Then there were the stairs. The Vicarage was built on vertical lines. On the ground floor was a kitchen and some storage. Then, up two runs of tall solid oak plank stairs brought you to the first floor. Here there were two bedrooms, a small, regular equipped bathroom off a hall and a large bathroom with multiple stalls and showers intended for larger groups. In the corner on this floor, was a very large open sala or living room. It had commanding views over the Cathedral. All the floors were wide solid wood planks. The walls were plaster and the ceilings were a combination of huge old-growth wood beams and carved wooden arches. From an architect's perspective this is a truly a magnificent building.

I was first shown the Vicarage in late August 2016 when it was being considered. My comments to the Pilgrim Office staff were that in the U.S. this was a million-dollar view. You could not pay for a building with a location like this to renovate. And if you could, the renovation costs would be several millions of dollars.

Another two full runs of oak plank stairs brought you to the second or topmost floor. Here there were three bedrooms, one normal bathroom with a tub, and a full kitchen. There were a small dining area off the kitchen and a large hall. The single best feature of this floor was that one of the bedrooms contained a large, matrimonial-sized bed and the window looked down on the Cathedral.

There was no internet at all, but the cellular coverage from the corner windows was great, at least from the window sills. Inside the structure, the signal dropped off as the near meter-thick granite walls tended to block phone signals. There were also precious few electrical outlets.

Another thing I noticed is that there was no heating source. No fireplaces, wood stoves, etc. There were a variety of electric space heaters around. But I immediately realized that this place would be very cold and damp in the winter months. As I only volunteered in July and August, this was not a concern. Plus, even in the hottest months, the very thick stone walls kept the inside temperature reasonable.

We were assigned rooms and I was lucky enough to be assigned the room looking down on the Cathedral with the large bed. This proved to be a most excellent vantage point for watching the fireworks over the Cathedral for the Feast of Santiago on the evening of 24th July. It was much quieter than the previous flat above the train station where I had stayed the two past years.

Here in the Vicarage, there were primarily three problems:

1. It was steeply uphill to get there from the Pilgrim Office. This caused my knees to hurt as they did on Camino. I found a less steep workaround by walking the opposite direction up to the Parador, then to Plaza Cervantes, turning left there, and one of the back streets took me to the Plaza San Roque, about a block from the convent.

2. Those DAMN BELLS! The Clarisas are up early every morning. They have a daily prayer routine that includes a call to prayer at 06:30 am every morning. The bell in the convent church tower has a particularly high note as compared to the Cathedral bells. Every morning

exactly at 06:30 am the bells start to ring. It is only one bell, but clang, clang, clang, clang - for maybe three minutes. Whichever Clarisa is pulling that rope must have really well-developed arm muscles. I like to sleep until 8:00 am, when left to my own devices. However, when staying at the convent, EVERYONE is up at 06:30 am.

3. To top this off, the local church picks up on this routine at 6:45 am each morning to signal people to come to the 7:00 am Mass celebrated in the local church just across Avenida San Roque from the convent. You can't win.

Aside from that, living in the convent was a pleasure. The groups of volunteers bonded like a family and worked together to keep the place orderly and neat. On occasion we would have homecooked meals. We looked after one another and helped as needed.

To this day, my only lingering doubts about staying there when I volunteered were the hills and stairs. My knees could not handle them. This was explained much earlier as relating to several decades of being morbidly obese. But, by 2017, even walking one kilometer on hard granite paving stones then up the stairs caused me pain. I had to revert to my Camino walking knee preparation routine of pain relief oral medication, topical creams and elastic knee braces.

By 2017, I was also using a hiking cane each day to walk up and down the hill. It helped relieve some of the pressure on my knees.

48

El Sherif

Santiago de Compostela, Galicia, Spain

July 2017 (V)

During my volunteer service from mid-July through mid-August 2017, we were still using the classic FIFO (first in / first out) queueing system. Arriving pilgrims got on the end of the queue and waited for their turn to be interviewed at the counter in the office. This is more or less the same system that had been used for decades.

In the off-season, or even early in the morning during the summer season, it was frequently possible to arrive at the office and enter the office to be interviewed with virtually no queue. Conversely, by midday, and especially once the noon Pilgrim Mass let out in the Cathedral, it was common for the waiting time to surge to two hours or more.

The previous year, 2016, one of the security guards commented to me that "Whenever you work, everything runs smooth and orderly, we have no problems with the queues. You are like the sheriff." Okay, compliment acknowledged.

I do have a knack for managing people in a queue. This likely stems from my early professional career as a civil servant working in processes that were virtually identical to how the Pilgrim Office processes arriving pilgrims. I understood the psychology and behavior of people in a queue. I knew how to keep them motivated, entertained and well-behaved.

Chapter 48

When I returned to my Florida home in August 2016, I did not forget the comment about "El Sherif." During the off-season, I did some research on the entire subject of a Sheriff in Spain and how I might be able to incorporate the concept in 2017.

I learned that, while the North American concept of a Sheriff as a law enforcement official stems from English common law, in Spain, it stems from the Arabic term 'el sherif.' In the Mozarabic context that existed in Spain for hundreds of years, the term took on a similar meaning as an official-in-charge. However, instead of originally being an officer of a court, the sheriff was more akin to a local lord or person of some standing who enforced the dictates of his overlords.

This was all very well and interesting. One day I decided to try to find a replica Sheriff's badge. In a local party supply store, I found a package of silver metal stars that had five points and the word "Sheriff" molded into the metal.

In a brief moment of inspiration, I found some Camino-related lapel pins I had at home. Using my drill to create a hole in the correct place, I managed to mount a red Cruz de Santiago lapel pin in a way that covered the second "f" in Sheriff. I used Super Glue to mount the pin securely. Now the badge said "Sherif," with a red Cruz de Santiago pin appearing to be part of the badge.

So was born 'El Sherif.' When I returned in mid-July 2017 to work again as a volunteer, I pinned the five-pointed star to my Voluntario t-shirt. The security guys found it hilarious, as did the staff. My fellow volunteers thought it was cute. But the pilgrims, well, many of them actually thought the badge was real.

This last notion made keeping things orderly even easier than it had been. Previously, I might have to plead or cajole some pilgrims to move over or forward, or to turn the line a certain way to get people into the shade or out of the rain. Now, with the badge, I only had to ask once, politely.

Whenever any pilgrim, or even the local police officers would see me, I was quick to point out that this was una broma grande, a big joke, for the pilgrims.

The really neat thing about this is that I became known simply as El Sherif by the Pilgrim Office staff, the Cathedral authorities, and anyone doing business there. Over time, when I told people to ask for something when they got to the counter, I would tell them to say that El Sherif told you to ask for this or that.

It turned out to be a win-win for all.

49

Dr. Santiago Fernandez

Monforte de Lemos, Galicia, Spain

April 2018 (P)

My intended Camino in 2018 was to walk the Camino de Invierno, the Winter Route, to determine if it made sense as a potential detour or alternative to avoid the crowding on the final segment of the Camino Francés. Many of us Camino veterans were wondering if doing this as an alternative to the foreseeable crowds for the coming 2021 Holy Year might be a good idea. A number of us took up the challenge to re-trace this route and make sure the guide books were all updated.

From Ponferrada, the traditional route of the Camino Francés took about 210 kilometers and about nine days. Conversely, the Camino de Invierno was about 40 kilometers longer and would nominally require an extra two days walking. It seemed like a good idea. Plans were made, plane tickets purchased and off I went.

Starting from the Saint Nicholas Albergue in Ponferrada, one turns to the right to continue on the traditional Camino Francés to O'Cebreiro, Sarria and onward to Santiago de Compostela. To start the Camino de Invierno, one turns to the left, walks to the next corner, at the cruceiro (stone cross) and turns left. Almost immediately, you pick up mojone distance markers for the Camino de Invierno.

Although the Jacobeo (Xacobeo in Galicia), the group

overseeing all things Camino in Spain, did not approve inclusion of the Invierno as a traditional / historic route until 2016, it is very well marked. The interesting thing is that when you start the Invierno, you are in the Province of León, but in the autonomous region called El Bierzo.

In this area, slate mining has been a long dominant industry. The houses all have slate tiled roofs instead of the traditional red clay tile roofs so prevalent across most all of Spain. One offshoot of this is that the mojone distance markers are built of black slate stone. They look pretty much the same as all other stone mojones, content-wise, on other Camino routes. But here they are a black stone material.

Not until you cross the River Sil into Galicia do the mojone distance markers become granite. Granite is the predominant stone quarried in Galicia, so this is understandable.

In 2018, I started at Ponferrada. But by the time I had walked four days to Quiroga, my right heel was acting up again the same way it had given me a serious problem in 2013. The callus on my right heel was thick, and there was a blood pocket under the thick dead skin. It was increasingly painful to walk.

Having dealt with this exact problem on the Camino Francés at Burgos in 2013, I knew exactly what I had to do. Except NOW I had converted over to using a proper smartphone, an iPhone 6s, so I had data access.

The first thing I did was to use Google Maps to query "podiatrist near me." BAM! The results came up, arrayed on a map according to the distance from my location. Believe it or not, the first name on the list was a Dr. Santiago Fernandez in my destination city for that day, Monforte de Lemos. Now, what are the odds of that occurring, seriously? Right off, I figured the gods were smiling on me. Either that, or I had Santiago himself as a shadow.

Chapter 49

The second thing I did was to pull up the RENFE train app to see if and when there was train service from Quiroga to Monforte de Lemos. It was presently early morning and there was a train at 11:00 am and another in the afternoon. Success! So far, so good.

I knew I had a reserved hotel room at Monforte, as I was intending to walk some 36 kilometers to get there. But clearly, plan A was a non-starter. It was already rather late in the morning to start walking that far. Plus, with my foot protesting, it would take far longer.

On to Plan B. I dialed the phone. When a gentleman answered, I asked if this was the office of Dr. Fernandez. He said "Sí." Knowing I was fast running out of functional Spanish, I asked if he spoke English. My Guardian Angel was definitely working overtime, because he said, "Yes, a little."

I slowly, and using as much Spanish as I felt comfortable, told him that I was a pilgrim on the Camino de Invierno, I was at Quiroga and needed his help. I was able to explain that "I had callus on my right-foot with blood."

He asked if I could get there today. I told him I could take the train at 11:00 am from Quiroga. He said to come to his office at 13:00 and he would see me. Excellent, I had a viable way forward!

I finished my coffee at the café across from the train station and made the train on time. Some 20 minutes later I was exiting the train at Monforte de Lemos. I disliked using transportation to leap frog over Camino segments, but I was also a firm believer that "needs must." A pilgrim must adapt and overcome when presented with challenges. Besides, as Monforte de Lemos was still about 134 kilometers from Santiago, my chance to get a Compostela was still in play.

Using Google Maps again, I navigated to my reserved hotel.

I considered myself very lucky to find out it was actually on the way to the doctor's office. The hotel was able to check me into my room and I was ready to go see the doctor named Santiago.

Shortly before 13:00, I walked two blocks, then left another block to find the address. I rang the bell, identified myself and was admitted.

Dr. Santiago Fernandez was a younger doctor than the other fellow who had helped me five years earlier. But as he had some English and I had a tiny bit of Spanish, we were able to get down to business. He had me strip off both boots and socks, and sit in the chair.

For the next 30 minutes, he hummed softly to himself as he carved away at my right heel, after prodigious amounts of lidocaine I must add. Don't ask me why, but sitting back in the chair which resembled a dentist's chair, I felt compelled to take a photo of the good doctor bent over my foot doing his thing. I show this to people, even now, to prove that this occurred.

When he was done, he pronounced the job excellent. He gave me a prescription for an antibiotic and a medicated ointment to apply twice daily to the affected area. I asked him if I could walk tomorrow. He advised taking one rest day. I did. The hotel had the room, so I stayed the extra night. If you have the time, Monforte de Lemos is a very interesting little city to visit.

On the second day I headed for Chantada.

50

Bringing Coal to Newcastle
Belesar – Chantada, Galicia, Spain

April 2018 (P)

When I started writing this book of stories from and about the Camino, I began by making a largely chronological list of all the stories I could remember from my seven years walking Caminos and working as a volunteer at the Pilgrim Office in Santiago de Compostela. The title of this particular story was written down, as I clearly had something specific in my mind at that time.

Obviously, I forgot what that original thought was. It took several months working on this manuscript before I had a sudden epiphany about what it was that I was thinking about when I first wrote this title down.

One day in March 2020, after I had been writing stories occurring before and after this one, it suddenly came to me, WINE! I meant to write a story about wine and the Camino de Invierno. Then it finally dawned on me what that was all about. Talk about a senior moment.

Okay, here's the story. I am on the Camino de Invierno in April 2018, the day I left Belesar headed for Chantada. I walked up out of the valley of the River Minho. I had learned at the beginning of the Camino de Invierno that it was a lot less developed than other more popular pilgrim routes. Practically speaking this meant fewer cafes, albergues, shops, churches and other places of business where one might ask for a rubber stamp, or sello, for one's pilgrim credencial.

One of the particular challenges of walking the Camino de Invierno, at least in the spring of 2018, was that finding places that had sellos was like a scavenger hunt. Outside of the final 100 kilometers before Santiago, the minimum requirement was one sello daily, once you hit the 100-kilometer threshold, the requirement changes to two sellos daily. Normally, this is no big deal. You will typically obtain one sello wherever you sleep for the night, then you simply get another at some café or bar you stop at along the way.

The Camino de Invierno is the most scenically beautiful Camino I had yet walked. On the other hand, it had the least availability of places to get a sello. A pilgrim had to be creative.

As I got almost to the top of the valley leaving Belesar on the way to Chantada, I spotted a nice-looking building with a sign out front proclaiming it to be the Bodega La Romana. In plain English, this was the La Romana winery. There was a car parked out front and it looked like there were lights on inside. I figured, why not. It's worth a try.

I entered the building to determine that it was a wine shop and winery office. A man inside welcomed me and I asked him "Tienes un sello?" Do you have a stamp? He answered in English, "Of course!" Whew, success!

He offered me the use of the bathrooms, I accepted. When I came out, he was standing behind a bar, preparing two red wine glasses, pouring a red wine into each glass, a generous portion I might add.

This fellow says, "You must try this red wine." "But, Señor I say, it is too early in the day and I must walk to Chantada today." "No problem," he says, "the terrain is gentle from here, and this wine is light. I will have some, too. It would be impolite to let you drink alone." What could I do, but say, "But of course! Thank you very much for your hospitality."

As we enjoyed the wine, and it was a most excellent red varietal wine, he proceeded to tell me about the history of the Ribeira Sacra, how the Romans had planted the first grape vines brought from Italy, over 2,000 years ago, and how the unique soil and weather conditions here in the Ribeira, along the valleys formed by both the rivers Sil and Minho, resulted in unique wines that were valued around the world.

He explained that there was an American man who owned three restaurants in San Francisco, California, who came here each winter to sample the new wine and to buy wine by the pallet. Yes, that is correct, he bought pallet lots, with each pallet containing about 96 cases of wine, 12 bottles to a case. The pallets were shrink-wrapped. That's a LOT of wine.

This fellow went to wineries up and down the valley selecting those wines he wanted to offer in his San Francisco restaurants. He would typically buy several pallet lots of wine from each winery after he had selected the wines he would buy.

Deals were done, and some days later a truck would pull up to each bodega. The shrink-wrapped pallets were loaded and stacked, into a full-sized 40-foot / 12-meter container. This container was then trucked to the coast and placed on a ship to bring the wine from Spain to San Francisco.

I told the man I was very confused. I explained that just north of San Francisco, just across the bay, are the counties of Napa and Sonoma. These counties have been producing world-class wines in most any varietal grape available for some 150 years. He said that he had not been to San Francisco but knew all about the wineries and wine growing industry in Napa and Sonoma.

He went on to say that although it might not make sense,

bringing very good wine to a region, internationally known for producing very good wine, there was a secret. Leaning close to me over the bar, he lowered his voice and said to me conspiratorially, "But señor, we have here, only here, in all the world, the special combination of soil, climate and sun that enable these particular varieties to grow here, and not anywhere else in the entire world."

He explained that the red Mencía, white Albariño and white Godello grapes only grew here as well as they do. That is the secret. They do not grow well or produce as fine a wine anywhere else but here in the Ribeira Sacra.

THAT is what I meant about a restauranteur from San Francisco "bringing coals to Newcastle." That phrase is an idiom that appears in several forms in several languages. It means to do or bring something superfluous or unnecessary, as in running *a lawn sprinkler when it is raining. This metaphor or idiom has been in use in English, since the mid-1500s. In French, the idiom states that doing something is like "bringing water to a river."*

Anyway, back to the story, and three glasses of two red wines later, I bid my very helpful host a fond adios. With sello in credencial and a light head, I continued on and eventually found Chantada. It was there all the time, exactly where it was supposed to be.

Of course, it did take me a fair amount of extra time to make those final kilometers. I never drink that early in the day. Fortunately, I had a fair amount of water with me. The combination of that much wine, I estimated it to be almost a full 750 ml bottle by the time I finished three generously poured glasses, plus the several liters of water I drank, had me 'watering the grass' multiple times in the hours it took to find my way to Chantada.

On the plus side of this argument, having to exert myself as

I did, likely prevented a hangover headache the next morning. I made certain to drink a lot of water and NO ALCOHOL that night. Still and all, it was a pleasant afternoon wandering in the sun with a slight buzz on.

Ah, these are the halcyon days we long remember.

The Heart of Stone
Belesar, Galicia, Spain

April (P) & July 2018 (V)

This first part of this story actually occurs the same day I happened on the bodega / winery while on my Camino in the previous story. The second part occurred some three months later, during my annual volunteer stint.

Leaving Monforte de Lemos on that second morning after my foot surgery, my feet felt very good and I was hopeful that I could complete the rest of this Camino more or less as planned. While I was at the pharmacy buying the items the doctor had prescribed, a young lady working there convinced me to invest in another pair of insoles, this time with gel inserts.

The irony is that they were Dr. Scholl's brand gel insoles. Though a major brand in the U.S., I had never before seen their products in Spain. But they fit well and made walking like being on a foam mat, very comfortable.

One of the dominant aspects of the Camino de Invierno is how it traverses valleys, up and down, to cross the River Sil and River Minho on many bridges. A typical day might include walking several kilometers down to arrive at a bridge across the river. You cross the bridge to walk up again, usually out of a valley. This process repeats itself across the river valley and through the region known as the Ribera Sacra. Each climb up or down is only maybe 300 meters, but doing it twice a day is tiring.

In this area, growing grapes for wine making has been an industry for several thousand years. In fact, many of the hillsides leading down to the rivers Sil or Minho have terraced vineyards with grapevines that were first planted during Roman times. That these vines continue to produce excellent quality grapes is amazing.

On a sunny morning, I am walking up out of the hamlet of Belesar through these terraced vineyards on a winding road with switchbacks. According to my guidebook, an original Roman road splits off forming a shortcut to get to the top of the windy road climb. I locate and take the cut-off for this Roman road.

The road is more of a rocky path. But I can see the stone wall to one side that formed a barrier at one time. Whenever I walk up, I place my hiking poles very intentionally and tend to look down so I can see where my feet are going.

About 50 meters up the road / path, my eyes spot something unique on the ground. Here is the photo I took:

Okay, You tell me, what did I just find? The photo does not show the size and mass of the Heart of Stone. It was approximately the size of an actual human heart. It weighed at least a kilogram. I know because I lifted it, then put it back where I found it. I thanked my luck for having gotten the photo and walked on.

That evening, at my hotel in Chantada, I sent my wife a copy of the photo using e-mail and the hotel's Wi-Fi. Remembering the six-hour time difference between Spain and my U.S. home, I did not see my wife's reply until the next morning when I was having a light breakfast before walking to Rodeiro.

She was amazed at the beautiful stone I had found, thought it incredibly romantic, and commented that it would make a fine addition to the family room collection of items from our world travels. Uh-oh! I think I stepped in it.

I had to patiently explain that I was already some ten or more kilometers beyond the point where I found and photographed the stone and that I could not return to fetch it. I went on the explain that I was a pilgrim. We do NOT pick up heavy stones like this. In fact, we leave stones at places like Cruz de Ferro. I explained that even if I was so inclined, there was NO WAY I was going to carry that heavy rock across Galicia.

Let's just say I got a very dissatisfied 'pout' from 6,000 kilometers (4,000 miles) away.

When I returned home in May, I discovered that my wife had printed the photo in color and had it professionally framed. It still hangs on the wall in our living room. However, it continued to nag at me that I had not brought that special stone home with me.

Okay, now we can fast forward to several months later in July, when I returned for my annual volunteer assignment. After checking in and being assigned my room at the convent up the hill, I spoke with Peter, one of the British volunteers I had worked with the previous summer. We got on great and always enjoyed working together.

I asked Peter if he was up for a special road trip. He asked why. I explained the above story and told him that I intended to rent a car and find that stone if it was possible. I explained that I had learned after going home that all iPhone photos are automatically time and date stamped, and the exact GPS location is also added to the photo information. Then I told him I had figured out how, and retrieved the GPS location information.

Using my iPhone, I opened Google Maps and copied into it the GPS location I had saved as a note. Immediately the location on the old Roman road in Belesar popped up, with a blue dot marking the stone's location when it was photographed some three months earlier. Peter was intrigued. I ordered a car for our first day off, several days hence.

We got the car from the Enterprise location next to the train station and headed out in the early morning. It took about 90 minutes to drive to Belesar. Funny thing, but everything looks a lot different when you are in a car driving backwards along some of the same country lanes and farm roads I earlier trekked on.

The blue location dot in Google Maps led us to park the car at the top of the Roman road. The road segment was perhaps 100 meters long and I had found the stone nearer the bottom. We got out of the car and walked slowly from top to bottom. It was difficult to watch the blue dots converging and also watch for the stone. I asked Peter to take the phone and give me directions like warmer…warmer…colder… as the two dots converged or diverged

As we slowly stepped down this road, we noticed that there was a lot of evidence of powerful water runoff, from the paved road above to the paved road below. Peter indicated that he had heard that the spring had been very wet with a lot of very heavy rainfall. I commented that water always finds the path of least resistance, and that a straight line down this Roman road was more efficient than flowing down a winding farm road. We needed to allow for that factor.

After about ten minutes the blue dots converged. Peter stated that here is where the stone was supposed to be, but was not. We looked from side to side and off the road, nothing.

It occurred to me to factor in the water runover variable. I told Peter that he should remain where he was to mark the exact, original location. I would start at the bottom of the old road and slowly make my way back up the hill in an "S" pattern.

It took a further 15 minutes, but off the west side of the road I spotted a stone of about the right size. Getting excited, I stepped over and bent down. SUCCESS!

The Heart of Stone had apparently been beat-up by the water runoff and washed some 30 meters or so down the trail and pushed off to one side of the road. Had I been walking a Camino coming up that road as I had some months before, I would have never seen the stone. It was on its side, hanging off the road.

We took the stone back to Santiago. I used up one of my Oral B electronic toothbrush heads to clean every nook and cranny of this stone. Then I went to one of the local China shops to buy a small wooden box to hold the stone. I took it to the office and showed it around. All the women thought it incredibly romantic. The men thought it was a rock.

Packed to go, I hand-carried this stone all the way back home at the end of my 2018 volunteer assignment and presented it to my wife.

Many of you may know the adage: "Happy Wife, Happy Life?" Well, let's just say my wife was very happy to have the actual rock. She forgave me not carrying it in my rucksack when I originally spotted it.

And THAT my friends, is the true story of the Heart of Stone.

Psst, Want a Photo – El Payaso?
Santiago de Compostela, Galicia, Spain

July 2018 (V)

When I started working as a volunteer at the Pilgrim Office in Santiago de Compostela, and once the staff determined that my Spanish was not up to carrying on an unstructured conversation with a native speaker, a very wise decision was taken. In 2014, management decided to assign me to do "todas las otras cosas" all the other stuff, basically, everything else, except interviewing arriving pilgrims for Compostelas.

I was fine with this, and each year, since 2014, my Spanish has improved a little. I know that one of these years I am going to walk in and find myself holding up my end of a conversation with the staff. That might just lead to my being assigned to interview pilgrims.

This is both a good and bad thing. It is good, because I am there to help in any way I can. But it is a negative, in that I am enjoying all the miscellaneous activities I do in support of the basic mission of welcoming pilgrims and assisting them with whatever they need.

Among the things I do on a daily basis, and that I find so rewarding is meeting pilgrims as they exit the process from the office with their new Compostelas and Distance Certificates. One of the very common practices among these pilgrims is to want to take photos to celebrate the event. Most every pilgrim with a smartphone or camera wants a photo of themselves, or their group, sometimes holding their certificates and sometimes not.

Over the years I have developed a practice that I have become known for. I have found that offering to take a photo, "¿Quieres una foto juntos?" (Do you want a photo together?) is a great icebreaker.

Many pilgrims just assume I am trying to sell them something, as though this was a theme park. I assure them that, "No, es gratis – no, it is free." I turn my back so they can see the "Voluntario" text printed on the t-shirt, indicating that I work there as a volunteer. Then they are willing. I use their smartphones or cameras to take the desired photos using several backdrops that I have found over time work well depending on the time of day and the sun's position.

After the first year or two, I found an innovative way to compel these pilgrims to laugh when their photo is taken. In the U.S. and in some other countries, a large pharmacy chain and other retail businesses support national children's cancer charities by selling bright red foam rubber clown noses to raise money. They proclaim one day in May each year as Red Nose Day.

I now buy a dozen or more of these clown-like noses and bring them with me to Santiago de Compostela each year. This is a cost I choose to take on myself. It is simply what I do. I always have one used red nose in my pocket, and several unwrapped new ones in a cargo pocket of my pants.

When I have the nose on, I am El Payaso – the clown. But, where this really comes into play is when cold, wet, tired, stinky, unhappy pilgrims come out of the Pilgrim Office. Teenagers with parents, where the unamused teens really did not want to be there in the first place, dragged along spouses, people with injuries, etc.; these folks do not necessarily want to smile. I have a guaranteed cure for that sullen condition.

I first offer to take photos, establish that it is free, then choose a suitable backdrop. Depending on where this occurs, it might be on the street in front of the Pilgrim Office, in the central garden courtyard where there is a beautiful water fountain, or on the terrace overlooking the rear garden.

Once the spot is selected, I have to wait until all the stragglers emerge from the certificate process and are present. When everyone is present, I arrange them to include everyone in the photo holding their certificates or not.

When I have everyone sorted and arranged, I accept the first of the smartphones or cameras the group wants me to use. I practice with the focus, angle and vertical versus horizontal orientation. Also, I will ask the group what their setup preference is. Do they want to show feet, or from the waist up, vertical or horizontal orientation, etc?

Once this is all sorted, I turn away from them, I put my red foam nose on. Then, when I turn to face them with the camera coming up, they are all usually laughing uncontrollably – at me – by then. THAT is when I take the photo. It never fails. Crying children, moody teenagers, annoyed adults, surly spouses, people in physical or emotional pain, it does not matter. They ALL laugh.

I do not care that they may be laughing at me. That is the point. I do not care why they are laughing. My mission is to welcome the pilgrims. I take it very seriously. In my view, this includes sending them along on their journey after this process with a smile on their faces.

It is my firm belief that, later on, when they review the photos in the comfort of their home, or perhaps show friends and family, they will reflect on that moment as a special one, and hopefully a happy one. If this happens, then my efforts will have been worthwhile.

Another aspect of this effort is that sometimes a child, usually very young, or with special needs, determines that they just MUST touch my nose. I usually move in and make funny noises when they touch the nose. A beeping sound is usually the favorite. Sometimes, a small child will grab the nose.

That is when I move to plan B. I reach into my cargo pocket for a new cello-wrapped nose. After checking with the parents that the child, or a present sibling, is at least 3 years old, because of possible choking hazards, I offer a new nose to the child. I allow the parent to unwrap it so everyone can see that it is new out of the package. Then I exchange my old nose for the new nose.

I show both the child and the parent or responsible adult how to squeeze the nose to put it on without splitting the rubber. There is a right way and a wrong way to spread the nose to put it on. On the other hand, and as some of the younger European boys just see a red ball, they use it as a football / soccer ball. Sometimes, I have the parents or older brother or sister wear the nose.

I will even take photos of the kids wearing a nose. That makes the day extra special. And THAT is what it is all about.

53

Donating a Bicycle

Santiago de Compostela, Galicia, Spain

July 2018 (V)

Many times, a pilgrim will end their Camino at the Pilgrim Office at Santiago de Compostela and look for an opportunity to dispose of something they used but do not want to keep. Most often this is the hiking poles or wooden staff they used to assist their pilgrimage journey.

The reason is that the airlines will not permit these poles to be carried into the cabin as a carry-on item. The reason is simple. All of these poles have a hardened tungsten metal tip. This makes the pole, even when collapsed, a usable stabbing weapon in the aircraft cabin. In the post 9-11 security environment, this is one of the changes we must all learn to cope with.

A lot of folks who do not plan to check a bag when returning home will dispose of the poles at the pilgrim office. We accept these poles and sticks. The best of the poles are usually brought to one of several charities in town that can reissue them to pilgrims who are looking for free poles. The lower quality poles are simply recycled as scrap steel or aluminum

Wooden poles and staffs are handled differently. Believe it or not, there are some folks living in and around Santiago de Compostela who still heat or cook with wood or coal. Often these people are poor. A local charity comes by the pilgrim office periodically to collect these wooden sticks. The metal tips and any decorations are removed. The sticks are cut into standard, stove-length pieces. They are then given away to use as kindling or cooking wood. It makes sense to me.

One August day in 2018, a bicycle pilgrim from Germany approached me as I was greeting arriving pilgrims on Rúa das Carretas, in front of the Pilgrim Office. This fellow was dressed from head to foot in all the de rigeur clothing and gear for a serious long-distance bicyclist. Plus, unlike too many other cycling pilgrims we see, this fellow actually fit into his neck to calf stretch Lycra outfit. But, everything about him, including the bicycle he was holding spoke money – loudly.

He asked in English if there was a place where he could donate his bicycle. He had just ridden from Stuttgart, Germany, a distance of nearly 1,900 kilometers, if I recall correctly. But it is a seriously long bicycle ride no matter how you look at it.

I examined the bicycle quickly and assessed that it appeared to be a custom-made bicycle with all very high-end components. In past years, I had commuted to work and graduate school on a custom-made bicycle and, although my experience was decades earlier, I understood quality components when I saw them. And I respected what I was seeing. This bicycle was easily worth a couple of thousand Euros.

I had never heard of the frame-maker before. I asked the pilgrim about this. He explained that he had this bicycle for three years and it had served him very well. It was custom made, including the frame, which was designed and sized to his body. But now, he wanted to donate it to another pilgrim who might put it to good use.

We talked for a few minutes and I offered to mind the bicycle while he went into the office to get his Compostela and Distance Certificate. He did not express an interest in the distance document. But I convinced him that, having ridden so far, he would eventually appreciate the documentation of his accomplishment.

After some time, this fellow came out. He was now happy that he obtained the Distance Certificate. I showed him on my iPhone using Google Maps, how to get to the Pilgrim House on Rúa Nova. We have no formal relationship with this ecumenical, charity-run pilgrim drop-in center. However, on a day-to-day basis, we do try to work together. They also have one of the best donativo operations in all of Santiago. Over the years, the folks working here have become good friends. Besides, by that time an idea was forming in my mind. We bid each other Buen Camino and parted ways.

Several hours later, my shift ended and I walked to the Pilgrim House. There, I spoke with the managers of the center, and asked if a very polite German man wearing Lycra came by to donate a bicycle. They said yes, and that he was very cordial and happy to leave the bicycle. They also were very impressed that this was far better-quality bicycle than they usually receive in donation.

I raised my idea. We have a mutual friend, Miguel, who lives in Santiago, and who makes his living writing guide books and smartphone apps for most all the Camino routes. To accomplish this and to develop accurate distance measurements, Miguel mounts a GPS satellite sensor to his bicycle and saves very accurate track files for each Camino route. Several weeks earlier Miguel mentioned to me that he needed to find a new bicycle as his older department store grade bike was in its death throes.

The idea I pitched was that Miguel was helping all pilgrims through his efforts. He was not getting rich from the effort, and was still trying to develop his niche in the very crowded Camino guide book market. Would they agree to give Miguel first-dibs (first-refusal rights) on this bicycle? We all agreed that this was the sort of quality bicycle that he needed to continue to do his good work.

I sent a text message to Miguel, briefly outlining the quality build of this bike and told him that the Pilgrim House folks had agreed to give him first dibs. Later that day, or perhaps the next morning, he came by and was very impressed by this, almost gift from Heaven. I had been right when I assessed that Miguel needed exactly this sort of bicycle.

I learned a couple of weeks later that Miguel just took the bike to a good local bicycle repair shop for new tires and tubes and an overall mechanical tune-up and lubrication. Despite some minor surface scratches on the custom paint, Miguel ended up with a better bike for his Camino guide writing and smartphone app writing efforts than he could have afforded.

Success! I just love it when a plan comes together.

54

Curing My Knees – A Miracle?

Santiago de Compostela, Galicia, Spain

May 2019 (V)

The original plan for my 2019 Camino was to fly into Oviedo – Asturias airport at the end of April, take the bus to downtown Oviedo, and then walk the original and first official Camino route, the Camino Primitivo to Santiago de Compostela. However, no plan survives the first shot fired in anger. Of course, something just had to intervene to change my planning.

Three weeks before my planned April departure date, one of my doctors found a problem with my bariatric lap band installed on my stomach to help me keep my weight down since 2005. This problem was causing lightheadedness and the possibility of sudden onset syncope (fainting). This had happened previously in 2015 while I was on the Camino Portuguese between Porto and Santiago de Compostela. It is also featured in an earlier story about Dirt Naps. The doctor advised that going on Camino was not a good idea until we got this problem sorted.

Well, needs must, so I went home and contacted the folks at the ACC (Acogida Cristiana del Camino) at Santiago de Compostela to offer my services as a volunteer during the time I would have been on Camino. The doctor only said I could not walk long distances. He did not say I could not travel. An agreement was reached and my plans shifted fast.

I cancelled most all my reservations made to support walking the Camino, and extended my reservation at Santiago de Compostela for three weeks instead of a few days after my originally planned Camino. My ground travel plan was still to fly into the Oviedo – Asturias airport, as changing the ticket would have been very expensive.

I flew via Madrid into Oviedo – Asturias then took the airport shuttle bus into Oviedo, and got on another bus from the bus station there to Santiago de Compostela. There, my friend Sybille met me and we lugged all my stuff to my hotel lodgings.

Typically, I always bring at least two suitcases or duffel bags as I bring donativo items to leave at the Pilgrim House, or things that Sybille might need. I recall that on this trip I had some dozen trash picker-grabber devices that folded so they were easily backpackable. These were for use by Sybille and Rebekah Scott for her Ditch Pig, Camino cleanup program.

I got settled into my lodgings then went to the Pilgrim Office to get my schedule and assignments sorted. Since about 2015, I had been using a hiking cane to ease the stress on my knees. This was because walking on the hard granite paving stones and stairs all over Santiago de Compostela made them ache. Also, the place I was staying for my time there was uphill from the Pilgrim Office, in the Plaza de San Roque area. The cane would also be helpful propelling myself up and down the many stairs and very steep streets.

My volunteer service began, and I did pretty much what I usually do to help for the next couple of weeks. My last day of work at the office was to be Monday 20 May. This is significant, because that is when everything germane to this story actually happened.

At that time, we were still using a classic first in – first out (FIFO) queueing system. One of my duties was to keep this line orderly and moving smoothly. This included chatting with pilgrims and answering their many questions, offering any help I could. Another aspect of this was to identify groups of pilgrims.

Each day, the group office personnel will decide, based on workload, how many people constitute a group for that day, or until they say otherwise. This usually varies from a high of six or seven to a low of four. In reality, the number can vary throughout the day, based on workload.

On this Monday, I asked and was told that I could refer groups of four or more. This means that these arriving pilgrims could leave the FIFO line and be processed, offline as a group. The requirement was that all persons in the group have started their Caminos on the exact same date and at the same place (town). One person from the group is designated as the leader and completes an estadillo form, providing demographic information about each group member. This is the exact same form that all pilgrims are asked to fill in when they get to the counter.

As all the information for all the persons in the group is the same, this moves the overall process faster. This is because a bunch of pilgrim credenciales can be reviewed, double-stamped, and Compostelas completed far more rapidly than can individual pilgrim processing. Plus, the process occurs in a back room, out of sight of the pilgrims or others. It is not as personal as one-off processing but it does get the job done fast.

But, to make this work we first have to identify the group. On that morning, I was walking the line chatting with people when I noticed a fellow speaking with another pilgrim further back in the line. The content of the conversation suggested they might be walking together. I asked the first person if he knew the other pilgrim. He said, yes, they were a group of eight pilgrims who were walking together but who had started at different times this morning.

I explained the group process to this first fellow who was perhaps 20 minutes from being admitted for solo processing. He said there were three others from the group in line behind him, and another four in town on their way here. I asked him to text the four folks walking in, telling them to meet the group in front of the office. Then I asked him to have the other three behind him in the queue to raise their hands. I went to each and asked them to follow me.

Collecting the first four pilgrims, I grabbed a clipboard, an estadillo form, and a pen on the way, and we all went to the front lobby area. There are several tables there that can be used to write on. There, I suggested that the first pilgrim would be the leader, and I explained how he had to fill out the form for all the others, one pilgrim to each line, and that he needed to ensure their credenciales were properly filled in on the front cover. He was to collect the credenciales.

As I am doing this, I am chatting with the other group members. The second tranche of four had arrived and everyone was high-fiving and celebrating. As we talked, I learned they were a group of Americans from an evangelical church somewhere in the central part of the country. To this day, I do not know what city or U.S. state they were from.

We chatted. The form was completed. The leader took it into the group office and was given a receipt for the form and credenciales and told to come back at 1:30 pm to pick up the completed Compostelas, Distance Certificates, etc.

The group returned on time at 1:30 pm. I told the leader where to go to collect the certificates. The other seven, plus me, stood outside on Rúa das Carretas in front of the office. They were asking questions and I was answering them as best

I could. Photos were asked for and taken. I even used the red clown nose. Everyone had a good time.

As we were all standing there, a man approached a niche shrine behind us, set into the outer wall of the Pilgrim Office building. Contained in the shrine is a ceramic statue of the Blessed Virgin Mary. An engraved plaque just beneath the shrine niche identifies this as the shrine of *Nuestra Señora de los Remedios* (Our Lady of the Cures). Recall that I mentioned in an earlier story that this very old building had previously been used as a hospital or rehabilitation home for senior citizens. Immediately on the inner side of this wall was the original and ornate Chapel for this complex.

The tiny shrine is protected by iron bars. But hands can be put through the vertical bars and people leave notes, cards, flowers, candles, Rosary Beads, etc., there as devotions or prayer intentions.

Anyway, back to the man and the shrine. He made the Sign of the Cross, kissed his fingers, and reached in to touch the statue of the Virgin Mary. He then crossed himself once more and continued walking down the street.

One of the young women in the group saw this happening about six feet behind us and asked me, "What was THAT all about?" Okay, teaching moment, and away I went.

"You recall how I explained what this building had been used for before it was the Pilgrim Office?" "Yes," was the group reply. "Okay, allow me to explain. First, I have to establish a common understanding so I can better explain."

"Let me start off by my supposition that you all are from a protestant sect church back in the States." "Yes, we are from an evangelical parish." "Fine, I happen to be a 'Cradle Catholic' born into that faith tradition so I will explain."

"The first thing to understand is that Catholics do NOT

worship saints. We venerate them. Veneration is a form of honor and respect that is less than worship. I think that we can all agree that the First Commandment that we all ascribe to, establishes that all worship and glory is to God and in the case of the Trinity to His Son and the Holy Spirit or Ghost, whatever." Lots of heads bobbing up and down as a form of affirmation.

"Okay, coming off that understanding, we Catholics are taught that we can pray to a saint to ask that saint to intercede on our behalf with God the Father, God the Son, etc. This is acting as an intercessor for our request or prayer. I know that many, or most of our protestant brothers and sisters, believe in self-justification and praying directly to God the Father." More head bobbing up and down. "Okay, I get it. I totally respect that perspective. But it is really the same thing. You all may believe in direct access. We believe that an intercessor may make our case better than we can acting alone."

"Now, following that dogma of praying to a saint to act as a go-between or intercessor between you and the Big Guy, there is a hierarchy of saints. Some are regarded as being closer to God than others. Cutting his short, the Queen of all the Saints is the Blessed Virgin Mary, the mother of Jesus Christ. Let's face it, what Son is going to refuse something asked of his mother."

"Many Catholics, myself included, will pray to the Virgin Mary to ask her to intercede for us to her Son." As I am saying this, I am bringing out the large stainless-steel Immaculate Medal that I wear around my neck. I show it to them and point out that around the edge is engraved the words "Immaculate Mary, conceived without sin, pray for us who have recourse to thee." I explain this is a form of devotion that directs my prayers through the Immaculate Mary to ask for her help or intercession when we pray to God her Son.

Now, I have a group of eight genuinely interested people. I

shifted to explaining what just happened behind us. "That man who was just here was likely on his way to work, running an errand or something else. On his way he paused to say a prayer, given the history of this particularly shrine, likely asking for a cure for someone dear to him, or even for himself. He blessed himself as a way to introduce himself to Our Lady, uttered his prayer though he may have placed something in writing in the shrine, then he kissed the fingertips of the hand he blessed himself with to touch the statute as a sign of sincere respect. To close out the prayer, he blessed himself once more then headed on his way."

Now, this group had six women and two men in it. They were a genuine cross section of America. They were white, black, Hispanic, Asian, male and female. No two of them appeared to be of the same racial or ethnic group. They were arrayed around me in a semi-circle, much in the way a team might be standing around a coach.

One of the women sort of blurted out to me that she genuinely appreciated all the time I was taking, and how helpful I was, etc. I demurred and simply said, "Thank you, it's what I do. I enjoy engaging with pilgrims." Then she says, "Do you mind if we pray for you?" I mean what AM I going to say? No, thank you, seems boorish and just wrong. Thinking quickly, I just say, "Yes please, it would be an honor."

This group starts to move from being a semi-circle to a more encompassing circle. I am only a tiny bit more anxious because of the closing proximity of this group of eight people.

Then another of the six women from the other side of this group calls out, "Do you mind if we lay hands on you?" Okay, now this is getting into a weird zone. I lightly ask, "Can I keep my clothes on?" They all chuckle, as I say it, but I am nervous.

Then I have a "lightbulb moment." These folks are American

evangelicals who believe in faith-healing and the laying on of hands. Okay, I tell myself, this is how Jesus and his Apostles, including Santiago, cured people back in the day. What the heck, why not? Can't hurt, might help.

During our rambling conversation, they asked about my Camino history. During the discussion I did mention how damaged my knees were from decades of having been morbidly obese and that the menisci cartilage would not grow back. Clearly, someone was listening and paying attention.

Here, in front of the shrine of Our Lady of the Cures, four of the six women got on their knees, on the street. People, pilgrims and pedestrians were passing by likely wondering what the heck was going on. Two of the women each grabbed on to one of my knees. Two to the left knee, and two to the right.

I am standing in the middle of this group with my arms folded, feeling more than a little self-conscious. Frankly, I have no idea what to expect.

Then the praying starts. I don't mean a muted whispered prayer. I mean a roaring, wailing cry for Divine Intercession to cure my knees, to make my meniscus cartilage regenerate, something that medical science says can't happen.

This goes on for a full two minutes, I know because my eyes were watching the second-hand on my wristwatch. As the second-hand approaches two minutes the woman doing most of the loud weeping and wailing reaches a crescendo pleading "...in Jesus' name we ask this… AMEN!" Of course, I joined in to the Amen part. Everyone stood up, the people in the street resumed their passage this way and the other. During this impromptu revival prayer meeting, time sort of appeared to slow to a crawl. I offered my sincere thanks to these people. We wished one another a pleasant and safe journey home and the now standard "Buen Camino."

I must insert here that I have absolutely no idea who these people were, where they were from, apart from being fellow Americans, and that I helped them get sorted in the Pilgrim Office process, as it my job while I volunteer there. Names were never exchanged. It was very surreal.

We then separated, me back to my volunteer activities, and the group to wherever. I never saw or heard from them again.

I have previously mentioned that I had used a hiking cane to help alleviate the pain on my knees when I walked up and down the hard granite stairs and streets of Santiago de Compostela. I had used the cane when I reported for work that Monday, my last volunteer day in this stint. I used it that afternoon when I returned to my lodgings.

Here is where things really get strange. When I arose the next morning, the recurrent pain in my right knee was COMPLETELY GONE. I had some mild pain in my left knee, but less than the previous day. I had errands to run and people to meet that Tuesday, 21 May, and I continued to use the cane.

When I awoke on the second morning, Wednesday, 22 May, the pain in my left knee was almost totally gone. I thought this was a good time to test the hypothesis that this might actually have worked. I left the cane in my room.

When I returned to the U.S. the following day, I did not use the cane at all. In fact, I packed it in my checked luggage.

Before I left, I did share this experience with some of my friends in and around Santiago. I explained that, although I genuinely believed in the possibility of a faith-based cure, I did take after my namesake, the ever-doubtful Apostle Thomas. In that context, I was going to have to wait and see how this all played out. My friends were also open minded as to a faith-based cure, but I needed more proof, of course.

Since that last week of May 2019 through the writing of

this account in June 2020, I have had zero pain or discomfort in either of my knees. When I returned to work as a volunteer at the Pilgrim Office for another month from mid-July to mid-August, I did not need the cane. Since then, and until now, I have had no pain in my knees.

In December 2019, I had my annual physical examination. While there, I mentioned to my general practitioner that I would like to have my knees evaluated as I had surgery to trim the menisci cartilage several decades earlier and I wanted to see how I was doing in that regard. A referral was made, an appointment set up, and I went to see a knee specialist. I told none of my doctors about what had happened in Santiago the previous May.

On the day of my knee examination, the doctor took my complete medical history, and then shot x-rays of both knees, from four directions in his office. These days, x-rays are developed immediately. A short while later, the doctor asked me to have a seat while he discussed the results of his examination.

He said that aside from some slight arthritis, my knees both looked fine and I would not be a candidate for joint replacement for a very long time, if ever. Then I asked him about my menisci. He explained that X-rays are not the best screening technology, but he could see the outlines of the cartilage and from his perspective they looked normal for a man of 66. What? Normal?

After I had to have the cartilage in both knees trimmed on both sides during the 1990s, the orthopedic surgeon told me that I would likely have to have early knee joint replacement as the menisci does not regenerate naturally. Clearly, the results of my December 2019 examination are opposite the expected situation.

What is going on? Is this a coincidence, or a miracle? Who knows? I DO know that the next time I am at the Pilgrim Office, and I pass the shrine of *Nuestra Señora de los Remedios* out front, I fully intend to say thank you for whatever happened on that day in May.

One of the oft repeated sayings on the Camino de Santiago is that Santiago works in strange ways and sometimes his methods are just weird.

The Best Seat in the House
Santiago de Compostela, Galicia, Spain

24 July 2019 (V)

The 25th of July every year is the annual feast of Saint James the Greater (Santiago). This day was fixed for the commemoration of his martyrdom by beheading at Jerusalem in AD 44.

Subsequently, his remains were placed on the mixed trash pile located outside the walls of the city, as was routine, according to Roman norms of the time. One night, soon thereafter, they were removed from the pile by two of his supporters then transported to northern Iberia or present-day Spain by boat. There, they were interred in a Roman convert to Christianity family crypt on their farming estate on the present site of the Cathedral. The remains of the great Saint remained there until they were rediscovered in the mid-800's AD. This is the very condensed version of how Santiago's relics came to be interred under the Cathedral altar at Santiago de Compostela.

Over the years, Santiago was proclaimed the patron Saint and protector of Spain. Remember that Spain remains among the most Catholic of all the European nations. As a consequence, religious traditions run deep and are taken very seriously here. Santiago's name is revered.

Each year, there are HUGE celebrations in his honor on the 25th of July. There are religious celebrations and processions, special entertainment and general partying.

Annually, just before midnight on the evening of the 24th of July, there is an immense fireworks display, and in recent years a laser light show depicting the life of Santiago and the transition or transporting of his relics to the city that bears his name.

These fireworks are launched from the (mostly) stone roof of the Pazo de Raxoi (Rajoy Palace). This is the very large, palatial-looking building opposite the west facade of the Cathedral, across the Plaza Obradoiro. Completed in 1766, this French neoclassic building is presently the seat of the city council.

While the fireworks have been launched from the roof of this building in past years, there were recent news accounts pointing out some damage to the roof from exhaust plumes and concern about the potential for fire. It seems the fireworks display may be moved, as from 2020.

The well-done laser light show depicting the life of Santiago and movement of his remains to Santiago is projected on the face of the Pazo de Raxoi / Rajoy Palace. The fireworks commence about 20 minutes before midnight, and last through midnight to usher in the annual feast day of the Apostle Santiago on 25 July.

Because of this, revelers crowd the Plaza Obradoiro beginning early on the afternoon on the 24th of July. Local and national police have to close off the plaza early in the evening to limit the crowd size. Being in the plaza has been the best place in town from which to see both the fireworks and the laser light show.

However, this is not necessarily the best seat in the house for viewing these happenings.

In July 2019, while I was doing my annual volunteer service, one of my coworkers, a very jovial and gregarious woman named Lila, decided it would be a good idea for a group of us to have dinner at the Parador, followed by ring-side seats to view the fireworks and light show.

Names were collected. I was encouraged to attend so they could seat us boy – girl – boy - girl, etc. Usually, I remain alone at my flat in the convent with the window overlooking the Cathedral and quietly watch the fireworks before going to sleep. Eventually, twelve volunteers joined the group. The fixed cost, all-inclusive, was €70 per person. Yes, that is right, seventy euros per person, payable in advance. But the reason becomes apparent a bit later.

For those of you who do not know, the Parador is a five-star hotel located on Plaza Obradoiro and perpendicular to the Cathedral. Basically, moving counter- or anti-clockwise ninety degrees each time, from the west facade of the Cathedral, one sees the Cathedral, then the Parador, then the Pazo de Raxoi / Rajoy Palace. The fourth side of the Plaza Obradoiro is formed by an old granite building now part of the University of Santiago de Compostela.

The Parador was built as a royal hospital in 1499 to accommodate pilgrims traveling to Santiago. Even now, its formal name is Hostal dos Reis Católicos (Hostel of the two Catholic Kings), it is considered among the oldest hotels in the world. It is the fanciest and most expensive place to stay in Santiago. The restaurants there are of the highest quality.

In addition, each 24 July, the Parador offers a fixed-price, multi-course dinner, combined with reserved area seating in front of the Parador building. Here, you are directly on Plaza Obradoiro and literally directly under the fireworks and laser light shows.

And, so it unfolded. We had to meet at a security cordon at 7:00 pm to be escorted through the police barriers as a group, but only if our names were on the list. Once we walked to the perimeter of the Parador seating outside, we were again vetted.

Finally, once inside and greeted by the maître de, were once more confirmed against the names on the original reservation list.

After being vetted three times, I was getting both hungry and thirsty. Our group was shown to our family-style rectangular table in the lower, family-style, more casual restaurant. I suppose that had I worn black tie, we might have been seated upstairs in the really fancy restaurant. As it was, some of the women in our group were wearing very nice dresses. The rest of us were dressed in our finest Camino-casual cargo pants and polo shirts.

But, no matter. All the food came from the same kitchen and we all were served the same menu. I cannot remember what all the food was, but it was excellent. But there was a soup course, a salad course, a fish course, and a meat course.

Wine was unlimited, in red or white, which we knowingly chose one of and stuck to it. I don't know about you, but switching from white to red, or vice versa, never works out well for me. In any event, a twitch of the finger brought a waiter scurrying over with a refill. Similarly, the excellent Spanish bread was unlimited. If you are a connoisseur of bread as I am, you know what I am talking about. Spanish bread is simply the best.

All of this gluttony was followed by a coffee and dessert course, of course. I don't remember what dessert it was. I do remember that it was insanely rich, very filling, and almost too much to finish on top of that huge meal. But, in my world, there is ALWAYS room for dessert. I was brave and stuffed it in.

We did not get up from the table where we had been sitting and feasting until about 11:15 pm. We were seated about 7:30 pm. Even coming from a traditional Italian family, who revel in huge, endless family dinners, this was a record for me. Whew!

We waddled away from our table, and met at the main entry

lobby. There a staff member ushered us to seats outside.

All the others in the Plaza Obradoiro for the festivities had to sit on the granite pavers. We had upholstered chairs with high backs. I have no idea where they came from, but I could allow myself to fall asleep easily. The chair even had arms.

Next to me was a fellow volunteer and friend named Ingrid from Toronto. We commiserated over how uncomfortable it was to be so full. It was actually a little painful. As we were speaking, the lights dimmed about 11:30 pm and the laser light show started.

The laser light show was the same as it is each year, but is always entertaining. I usually see something new each year. At least this year I was seated about 100 meters from the display.

At about 11:40 pm the fireworks began, with musical accompaniment. After about five minutes of "oohs" and "aahs" from the crowds and us seated in front of the Parador, as the fireworks exploded above us, Ingrid started dancing around in her seat and swatting at her nicely coiffed hair with both hands. "What's in my hair, am I on fire?!" she exclaimed in excited panic.

I stood up to face her, and noticed that both of us had falling debris from the cardboard fireworks tubes that exploded in air, as well as cinders from the expended fireworks, raining down on us. It was all over my head and shirt. Ingrid had it all over her blouse and in her blonde hair. Some of the cinders were still glowing faintly as they fell from the sky.

After I assured her that, no she was not on fire, and explained what it was, she reached into her tote bag and pulled out an umbrella. I explained that might annoy the others around us. We got up and moved away from the others for the remainder of the fireworks show. But, the fallout, such as it was, continued raining down for maybe five minutes even after the fireworks finale. And it was truly a world class fireworks finale. My ears continued to ring for maybe fifteen minutes after the end of the show.

Yup! Definitely the best seat in the house! We were actually IN the fireworks display. All the noise and crowds were very draining for me. It was an excellent evening with friends and I enjoyed it all.

But, next year, I think I will take a pass.

"Don" Thomas

Santiago de Compostela, Galicia, Spain

25 July 2019 (V)

In the year 1499, a Papal Bull issued by Pope Alexander VI authorized the Catholic monarchs to build a hospital for pilgrims. In this Bull, it is said that "a brotherhood of both sexes, of any nation or province that they were and in any part of the world that were found, had to be instituted and ordered, at the service of the pilgrims to Santiago."

That "Brotherhood of the Lord Santiago" was located in the original hospital for pilgrims, the imposing building located in the Plaza del Obradoiro and where the Hostal de los Reyes Católicos is currently installed. On August 3, 1939, the brotherhood was elevated to the rank of Archconfraternity Ad Honorem by order of Pope Pius XII. On April 16, 1942, the same Pontiff renamed the brotherhood as The Archconfraternity of the Apostle Santiago.

The activity of the Archconfraternity has a large number of members in Spain and other nations. In recent years, there has also been an exponential growth in the pilgrimage to Santiago, with a notable increase in brother "cofreres."

Currently, the headquarters office of the Universal Archconfraternity of the Apostle Santiago is at the International Pilgrimage Center (Pilgrim Office) of the Cathedral of Santiago. The main purposes of the Archconfraternity are to:

- Promote the cult of the Apostle Santiago,

- Maintain relationships with the brotherhoods around the world and help their Christian life,

- Promote pilgrimage to the tomb of the Apostle Santiago,

- Ensure that pilgrims are well received and attended to while on pilgrimage on all routes leading to Santiago,

- Offer help so pilgrimage is an occasion of evangelization for pilgrims, their areas of origin and the city of Santiago,

- Collaborate with the Cathedral of Santiago to provide spiritual, cultural and material care for pilgrims, and

- Collaborate in the conservation of the religious and cultural heritage linked to Santiago.

Membership is generally by application and only with the sponsorship of two or more current members in good standing. However, something happened to me one day, on my way to do a chore.

One day in August 2018, I needed to speak with the secretary of the Archconfraternity about something or other. When I got to her office, two other volunteers were there. One was inquiring about joining. The other volunteer was already a cofrere (lay brother). The secretary told the prospective applicant that she would need two sponsors, and she then gestured to me. "Surely Tomás can be a sponsor for you?"

"¿Quién yo?" I replied (Who me?). I explained that I was not a cofrere. The secretary looked aghast and asked how is that possible? "You have worked here every year for five years. You come every year to work with us for a month. How is it possible that you are not a cofrere?" "No sé – I don't know." was my reply, shrugging my shoulders.

With that, the secretary states aloud, "Well, that is unacceptable. Fill out this form and I will take care of it." "What about sponsors?" I asked. "It will not be a problem. You must become a cofrere. You are the sort of person we are looking for."

I have been around the block enough to know when to keep my mouth shut. I accepted the blank membership application, said thank you, and went away. I later returned the completed form to the secretary.

Later that year, long after I returned home, I received a letter from the Archconfraternity office in Santiago telling me that I had been accepted for membership and that my induction ceremony would be on the Feast of Santiago on 25 July 2019.

Okay, now fast forward to 25 July 2019. I am about mid-way through my month's volunteer service at the Pilgrim Office. The secretary suggested that I might bring some nicer clothes as the ceremony was to be held at a special Mass. I had on a nice pair of slacks and a dress shirt. Since retiring, that is as dressed as I get.

As the Cathedral was closed for renovations, the Mass and induction ceremony would be held at the Church of San Viz de Solovio adjacent to the fresh food market in Santiago. This is the ancient church built on the site that tradition holds the hermit monk Pelayo lived. He is the person who rediscovered the remains of the Apostle Saint around 844 AD.

The special Mass was on the Apostle's feast day, 25 July. At the Mass, an oath of office was administered. Rather large bronze medallions on ornate red cords were bestowed. And an ornate certificate was also given to me.

Here is a photo of the medallion.

Here is a photo of the certificate:

You will note that, with this certificate, I have been awarded the Spanish honorific of "Don." Hence, my pseudonym, "Don Thomas." This is without meaning at home, or most anywhere else out of Spain. But it is nice to be recognized in a special manner. I use the term when I am in Spain.

* * *

I am choosing to end my storytelling here, for now. Each year, I have new experiences, meet new friends and experience more stories. Who knows? There might be a second book in my future. Thank you for joining in my experiences by reading this book.

Afterword
What Was This All About Anyway?

My acquired passion for the Camino de Santiago did not occur immediately. I had to first complete a full, long, traditional Camino route. In this case, my first pilgrimage was on the Camino Francés, the most popular of all the several dozen routes.

Even when I arrived at Santiago de Compostela as a pilgrim for the first time, I was overwhelmed by a variety of emotions and thoughts. During the journey, my thoughts were all over the place. Some days I could be quiet and contemplative, meditating or praying silently. Other days, I craved the companionship and camaraderie of other pilgrims. On still other days, I needed to help make someone else's day, journey and life a little better.

After I went through the customary pilgrim arrival routine at Santiago de Compostela at the end of May 2013, I was in awe of the city, its architecture, institutions, history, people, culture and everything about it. But, after about a week, it was time to come home.

When I did arrive home, I experienced a profound post-Camino period of depression. In the years since, I have come to understand what this was. For the time you are on Camino, you live in a bubble of sorts. Everything you need you carry in your rucksack. If you do not have it, you do not need it. If you should need something you do not have, you can usually obtain it in the next town. I slowly came to realize that the Camino was not about things. Things ceased to have a value beyond their immediate utility. Possessing more stuff meant nothing. In fact, the more you had the more you had to carry – your burden was increased.

More importantly than that lesson, was the profound lesson that getting someplace was not as important as HOW you got there, and WHO you arrived with. This final realization is summed up best in a framed saying my wife had waiting for me when I arrived home from my first Camino. I evidently said it to her in an e-mail, text, or on one of the rare occasions we spoke.

I am retyping it here,

> **"Life is an adventure. Learn to enjoy the journey.
> I have learned that the journey IS the destination."**

And THAT my friends, is the single biggest lesson I learned. I cherish the experiences I have had, the people I have met and friends some have become. All of my Camino experiences have become an indelible part of my life's experience.

I wish you all the same satisfaction.

BUEN CAMINO!

About the Author

"Don Thomas" is a pseudonym. There are precious few elements of personal privacy left in this world and I am simply trying to preserve those elements where and when I can. Some of you reading this book will, of course, recognize me. But I will share something about me.

This is my first book, at least one I have written for public reading. I am learning as I go along.

The photo of me was taken in 2016, on Rúa Das Carretas, directly opposite the Pilgrim Office. I confess to having gained a few pounds since then. But this photograph captures what I did then and now.

As I mention in these stories, I walked my first Camino, the Camino Francés, from Saint Jean Pied de Port, starting in late April 2013. Since then, I have walked the Camino Portuguese both from Lisbon and Porto on separate occasions, the Camino de Madrid, and Camino de Invierno. I do try to walk one Camino each year. However, in 2019, medical problems preempted this notion. I volunteered for a second period of time at the Pilgrim Office.

Follow-up diagnostic tests revealed the problem and indicated surgery to repair the problem. That surgery occurred in June 2019 and was successful.

In 2020, I was all ready to start the Camino Vía de la Plata, starting from Sevilla and walking to the north towards Santiago de Compostela, when we all were hit with a case of "Covidus Interruptus." The COVID-19 coronavirus caused a global pandemic and ended up with Spain being closed to all foreigners. The Camino was closed by the Spanish government. The Pilgrim Office closed for the duration. International air travel simply stopped.

Like many thousands of others, I reluctantly cancelled my travel. But Santiago will still be there when we all can return safely once again. He, and the Camino are eternal.

Buen Camino!

www.ingramcontent.com/pod-product-compliance
Lightning Source LLC
Chambersburg PA
CBHW050503160726
48003CB00001B/141